Street Violence in the Nineteenth Century

Street Violence in the Nineteenth Century:

Media Panic or Real Danger?

Rob Sindall

Leicester University Press
(A division of Pinter Publishers)
Leicester, London and New York

© Rob Sindall 1990

First published in Great Britain in 1990 by Leicester University Press
(a division of Pinter Publishers Ltd).

Editorial offices
Fielding Johnson Building, University of Leicester,
University Road, Leicester, LE1 7RH

Trade and other enquiries
25 Floral Street, London, WC2E 9DS

British Library Cataloguing in Publication Data
A CIP cataloguing record for this book is available
from the British Library
ISBN 0-7185-1345-2

Typeset by DP Photosetting, Aylesbury, Bucks
Printed and bound in Great Britain by Biddles Ltd.

Library of Congress Cataloging-in-Publication Data
A CIP record for this book is available from
the Library of Congress.

Contents

For Wendy, Rebecca and John

Acknowledgements

My thanks are due to the late Professor Jim Dyos who gave me much inspiration, and to Dr Richard Rodger who offered invaluable advice and encouragement during the writing of this book. Without the efforts of Margaret Fielding who really 'couldn't be doing with it' it would never have been typed.

The staff of the Library at the University of Leicester have been of great help and have never failed to rise to any challenge offered. I have never met an unhelpful archivist or librarian in my academic travels and my thanks are due to the staff of the Public Record Office, Kew; British Museum Reading Room; British Museum Newspaper Library, Colindale; Central Library, Leicester; Record Office, Leicester; Manchester Central Libraries; Brown, Picton and Hornby Libraries, Liverpool; and the Lancashire Records Office, Preston.

1. The Background to Street Violence

I

G.M. Young, in his classic work on the Victorian age, observed that, 'the real, central theme of History is not what happened, but what people felt about it when it was happening'.[1] It is on this premise that this study of 'perceived' outbreaks of street robberies is based. The perception was that of the middle classes and was generated not by observation of actual events but of newspaper reports of such events and of criminal statistics and court reports which were believed to reflect such events. Whether such events (i.e. street robberies) actually happened is not of central importance to this work and is a fact which will forever remain unknown. What is important is that the middle classes believed that they actually happened and that the consequences of this belief led to changes in the control structure of their society.

The middle classes were dominant in a society which from 1850 to 1914 saw its population double, its urban population treble, its national income treble, achieved economic world leadership and made scientific and cultural advances far beyond those which had previously seemed possible.

The growing feeling of general security and self-satisfaction of the middle classes which was engendered by the prosperity of the 1850s and which was fully developed by the time of the death of Queen Victoria should not deflect the reader from appreciating the trepidation with which they viewed the future during the first five decades of the century. The end of the war in 1815 and its neutralisation of the direct threat of revolutionary France did not deter the middle classes from reading Edmund Burke's *Reflections on the Revolution in France* (1790). Internal threats of revolution emanating in the form of Luddism, the agitation against the Six Acts, the early attempts at mass unionisation in the proposed formation of the Grand National Consolidated Trades Union and the growth of Chartism were defused by legislation which firmly placed the middle classes on the side of the establishment. The Reform Act 1832 did not enfranchise the entire middle classes but had been formulated to give larger political influence to the new industrial, commercial and middle-class urban elements. The Municipal Corporations Act 1835 allowed the middle classes a greater say in local government but more important was the Catholic Emancipation Act 1829 which repealed the Test and Corporation Acts. This gave the protestant non-conformists, of whom the backbone were the urban middle classes, full civic rights and allowed the rise of the Whig-Liberal movement and the spread of the Protestant ethic of work and success. Real political insecurity was never to recur in the nineteenth century. The Chartist risings of the winter of 1839 and spring and summer of 1848 were massive displays of social discontent but were not beyond the resources of the army and the middle-class volunteers to control. Similarly, the writings of the European socialists and the revolution in France in 1848 may have kept the establishment alert but never really threatened its position. The socialist riots of the 1880s and the growth of organised labour were disturbing but they only rocked the societal boat and never threatened to overturn it. This relative political security allowed the establishment to face phenomena which had always existed but had never before been faced – social problems.

Britain was undergoing a unique experience in leading the world in the space of four or five decades in the process of urbanisation. It faced a wholly new social situation which led to the spontaneous development of a social system without any other social model as precedent and with only the past to measure it against. The middle classes sensed and observed change but did not know where it was taking them or what the final outcome might be.

Not until the last quarter of the century could people begin to get the urban transformation into perspective and only in retrospect reflect that 'the concentration of population into cities was the most remarkable social phenomenon of the present century'.[2] With hindsight and the knowledge that conditions improved it is difficult to appreciate the foreboding with which social change was observed in the 1830s and 1840s when Thomas Carlyle referred to the 'Condition of England Question'[3] and when the Reverend Thomas Malthus, who had written his pessimistic *Essay on Population* in 1798, was a founder member of the London Statistical Society. A superficial observation of society revealed a host of social problems involving sections of the population which were either ill-used or un-used by society. Many of these problems were not entirely new. Children had long been exploited on farms, in cottage industry and in small workshops. Paupers, lunatics and criminals had always been cruelly treated. Disease and plagues had always posed a threat to urban concentrations and it is only a distorted romantic vision that sees a farm-worker's hovel as being domestic luxury compared to the urban slum dwelling. Suddenly, in the thirty years since the turn of the century, the problems had become magnified and concentrated, reflecting the magnification and concentration of the population. At the same time the industrial and agricultural revolutions had brought an improved standard of living and with it a new standard of expectations amongst workers, whilst the governing classes became more aware of the problems which were concentrated in the towns and began to nurture a belief that they could be solved. Not only convinced that they could be solved, the governing classes were becoming aware of the necessity of the solution of social problems if further political problems were not to ensue. Thomas Arnold asked in 1832, 'Has the world ever seen a population as dangerous ... as the manufacturing population of Great Britain, crowded together in their most formidable masses'.[4] The middle and upper classes had begun to turn their attention from political to social problems and to realise that the former were largely a product of the latter.

The proposed solutions to these myriad problems could be classified as reflecting the two main political trends of the period. Paternalism reflected the attitudes of the Old Tories in contrast to the reforming ideas of the Whig-Liberals and New Conservatives (Peelites). Such a classification is crude but allows some idea to be gained of the major trends running through this complex society which in the space of a few decades 'discovered' an endless list of social problems which it had to solve, with no experience or example to aid in the solution.

For many the only solution to these new problems was to revitalise the old paternalistic ways. Paternalism had been the basis of English life since the feudalism of the middle ages. It was only with industrialisation and urbanisation that it was stated as a social theory by such Victorian intellectuals as Thomas Arnold, Thomas Carlyle, William Goldstone, Benjamin Disraeli and William Wordsworth.[5] Paternalism was based on the benevolent use of the power of property and of the Church. The paternalists saw a simple solution to *all* the social problems of the time. Through the efforts of the landed property owners and the Church they would lead a moral and spiritual regeneration of the nation which would create a more Christian and stable society. Enlightened land-owners would employ happy and contented labourers and if the growth of manufacturing continued then the owners of urban property would also realise their duties and act as model mill and mine owners. Moral decay, and its outward signs in the form of crime, vagrancy and prostitution, would disappear under the influence of the Church of England which would be responsible for the education of the people. For property and the Church, acting in local spheres, to provide for the poor, deal with criminals and clean towns these institutions had to be supported and given authority. Thus paternalists supported protection, the return of the religious monopoly of the Church of England and were strong believers in the efficacy of capital punishment, whipping of beggars, flogging in the Navy and flogging in schools.

Paternalism was popular because it was simple and was belived to have worked in the past (that is, the middle ages). In this period of rapid change it gave the establishment something to cling to and believe in, which helped to quell their fear. But it was not the answer. The cities were not only creating problems but also the collectivist mentality which was to encourage the growth of central government, while at the same time producing 'those middling, mobile classes far too independent for paternalism's condescending ways'.[6]

The innovative, reformist trend in English society at this time comprised a wide spectrum of thought. This includes the Whig-Liberal intelligentsia (such as Lord John Russell and Sir Robert Peel), Radicals (such as William Cobbett, Sir Francis Burdett, Thomas Attwood and Edward Bulwer Lytton), dissenters, evangelical philanthropists, political economists, utilitarians, and the statistical movement. The centre ground of this reformers' spectrum tended to be occupied by free-traders, supporters of the new Poor Law and tended to be anti-trades union and anti-working-class radical. They were laissez-faire in their attitude towards trade, the factory laws and crime although they supported government intervention in education and sanitation. An education system and free trade would abolish the evils of long hours, bad sanitation, working-class agitation, improvidence and vice. The middle classes were to lead Britain and set the example for a thrifty and virtuous working class.

H.J. Dyos noted the unique position of London in the mechanism of social change in Britain and this is also apparent in the episodes of street violence with which this work is concerned. London was essentially uncharacteristic of the rest of the nation. However, London still took the lead in the exertion of influence on the culture and the self-consciousness of the nation through 'the press and the parliament, the twin organs of metropolitan influence and control', so that the metropolis was 'a great influencer in terms of tastes and values, of imagery and opinion, and of all the ways of managing – or struggling to manage – such novel entities as cities in full spate'.[7] Thus London, although atypical, became the barometer for the progress of the industrialisation and urbanisation of the whole nation. It was the model of experience on which public opinion was largely formed through the medium of the press and legislation enacted through the medium of Parliament. It is not surprising that the legislation was therefore often inappropriate to the whole country and the opinion was, at times, misguided.

II

One of the social problems which nineteenth-century society felt compelled to solve was that of crime and in order to place the panics of the second half of the century in perspective it is necessary to appreciate the nature and level of crime during the period.

From Table 1.1 it is clear that during the second half of the century there was a general decline in the number of persons per 100,000 population appearing before the courts.

Most writers on the subject[8] agree that the degree of violence associated with crimes also declined in the second half of the century. There is no single explanatory factor for these declines but the fact remains that the nineteenth century witnessed a decline in violence and that by 1890 the rate of indictable offences per 100,000 was down to 200, a rate considerably lower than that prevalent today.[9] The newspapers did not waste many column inches on street violence prior to the garotte 'outbreaks' of the 1850s. This does not imply that it did not exist. The committal figures show that the chances of being attacked were probably far greater in the first half of the century than in the second.

Table 1.1 Committals for indictable offences per 100,000 in England and Wales

Years	Annual Average Rate	Years	Annual Average Rate
1857–60	262.8	1881–85	226.1
1861–65	287.9	1886–90	201.8
1866–70	270.5	1891–95	186.1
1871–75	223.8	1896–00	163.7
1876–80	221.9		

Source: Annual Criminal Statistics tabulated by V.A.C. Gatrell, 'The Decline of Theft and Violence in Victorian and Edwardian England', in V.A.C. Gatrell, B. Lenman and G. Parker (eds), *Crime and the Law: The Social History of Crime in Western Europe since 1500* (1980), p 282.

Although declining in numbers, incidents of violence in the streets of the nineteenth century were still common. Henry Mayhew cited the main types of street violence as perpetrated by, 'the sneaking thieves who adroitly slip their hands into your pockets, or low, coarse ruffians who follow in the wake of prostitutes, or garotte drunken men in the midnight street, or strike them down by brutal violence with a life-preserver or bludgeon'.[10] Violent robbery was not a new phenomenon in the second half of the nineteenth century but its newsworthiness was. Pre-1850 most newspapers did have a column of reports on the cases heard before the courts but actual crimes (except murder) were rarely reported. Newspapers may have had court reports but not crime reporters. Following a series of 'daring and determined' robberies and the inactivity of the police, one reader wrote in 1843:

> These recent robberies have not been made sufficiently public; they should be recorded in the daily journals, that if the police sleep, others at any rate be awakened to a sense of danger in which their otherwise unguarded property lies.[11]

The attitude of the press certainly did change in the third quarter of the century to the extent that no one could have been unaware of any danger to property and that the police were not allowed to sleep. This is not to imply that criminal activity increased to such a great extent, merely that press activity was disproportionately awakened.

III

From within their industrial and urban social environment with its predominantly optimistic outlook on a life of security, respectability and sedentary occupation, the middle classes began to discern a transient sub-group in society which did not fit into the middle-class image of society and which did not seem to acknowledge or respect the goals and norms of middle-class life. Not only did members of this sub-group not accept the values of middle-class life, they actually threatened them. This section of society was named by the middle classes as the 'dangerous classes'. They were a spectre which haunted the middle classes, being partly real and partly illusory. The 'dangerous classes' were 'dangerous' as their way of life was the antithesis of security, sedentary occupation and respectability. The 'danger' ranged from that of being insulted by a ruffian whilst taking an evening stroll to the overthrow of middle-class society by revolution. These 'dangerous classes' consisted of the 'idle poor' and the 'criminal classes'. All three groups were indefinable (as the middle classes themselves elude exact definition) but were real enough to the middle-class mind. Their presence in society was believed to pose a constant threat to middle-class society. For the middle classes it was akin to living close to a volcano. The volcano was not merely a mental apparition (although few respectable people actually saw it) but did have a physical location in the 'rough' quarters of all major cities. The location changed as the old rookeries were driven through by street improvements, railways and slum-clearance schemes. As the middle classes vacated the centres of the cities and retreated from city life into the suburbs, the 'dangerous classes' moved in.

The volcano of the 'dangerous classes' was constantly bubbling and the middle classes learned to accept this and tried to ignore it. It bubbled within its cone and did not leave its geographical limits. Now and again it bubbled vigorously enough to cause concern and trickles of activity flowed into middle class area. Hence:

> The public mind of England awakes periodically, and with a start, to a sense of the danger it incurs by the presence of a large criminal population in the very heart of the community.[12]

and

> Of the existence of this life of savagery, running parallel with the ordinary life of refinement and civilisation, the public know little or nothing, except as may be forced under their notice by an act of violence or more than usual daring outrage.[13]

At such times it was impossible to ignore the volcano of the 'dangerous classes' and the likelihood of its eruption caused fear and panic to spread through the middle classes.

We are presented with a situation in which the central class in a society has a growing feeling of security in all aspects of life except that of physical confrontation, primarily on an individual level and secondly on a class level. From time to time this insecurity seemed to dominate temporarily the middle-class psyche. At such times, a contemporary observed, 'We rave against the evil, we abuse our rulers, we insist upon a remedy being found, we listen eagerly to every quack and philosopher'. After much illogical and superficial argument a plan would be made to solve the problem 'which is usually some ill-digested and unworkable compromise between old habits and new fancies'. The public would then grow tired of the subject, ashamed of its panic, satisfied with its remedy 'and go quietly to sleep again for another term of five or seven years'.[14]

T.B. Lloyd-Baker, addressing the Social Science Congress, held at Belfast in 1867, saw the panic and its aftermath, rather than the events which were supposed to have caused the panic, as the more interesting phenomenon and noted its transient nature. Having observed that 'the most violent feeling was aroused' by the London garotting episodes and the ruffianism of June 1867 he remarked that, 'the fashion of terror passed away as quickly as the fashion of garotting'.[15]

It was observed in 1862 that, 'the social consequences of this sudden and startling growth of crimes are far more serious than the results of any amounts of robberies'.[16] It is with these social consequences that this work is primarily concerned. The minor eruptions of the volcano are interesting; the major panics they caused are more so.

IV

V.A.C. Gatrell[17] has laid down three valid premises concerning the definition of crime which obtain from any criminological study. The first is that crime is a social phenomenon and so reflects the societal setting. If one agrees with Blackstone's widely-accepted definition of crime as 'an act committed, or omitted, in violation of a public law either forbidding or commanding it', then it is apparent that the definition of that which constitutes a crime is delineated by the laws of the country at the time it was committed. As laws reflect the soceity which made them and for whose benefit they were made, then it follows that the definition of crime must also reflect the society. Secondly, each era sets its own standard of 'sufficient' action against those who break the law and that such sufficiency is conditioned by policy, administrative constraints, social interests and public attitudes. An aspect of this premise to which Gatrell does not draw attention is the time-lag effect. Laws reflect society when they are made but may survive whilst society changes and may no longer fit the needs of the changed society. To accommodate this, society has adopted a mechanism whereby 'sufficient' action against those who break certain laws is deemed to be no action at all, as it is recognised that, although the law remains on the statute book, it is not suited to the society which has evolved. (A twentieth-century example of this non-enforcement being regarded as sufficient action is that of the laws concerning the dropping of litter in the UK.) Thirdly, the 'crime' which characterises a society is actually only that degree of unlawful activity which law-makers and enforcers perceive through the filters of their own social prejudices, interests and assumptions. All three of these premises mean that the definition of 'crime' is highly variable.

It is a contention of this work that the state, the law-makers, administrative constraints, social interests and public attitudes were the main determinants of the official criminal statistics and of the number of newspaper court reports and so of the perceived outbreaks of 'crime'. As law-makers make law-breakers it was the 'public' and 'public opinion' that made a criminal a criminal and it is widely acknowledged (and will be clearly demonstrated in Chapter 3) that the 'public' and 'public opinion' meant the middle and upper classes. An underlying assumption on which the research for this book was based was that public panics could exert a major influence on changes in the published statistics of street violence. Such changes are highly significant as the crimes with which this work deals are often regarded as the best indicators of lawlessness within a society. Several rating tests have demonstrated how highly on a scale of seriousness the public view robbery and many criminologists regard robbery statistics as the truest reflection of the level of criminal activity. Thus movements in the statistics which purport to measure the safety of the highway by indicating the frequency of such offences are crucial to society's assessment of its security and so figure largely in decisions concerning the tightening or relaxing of the instruments of security (e.g. police, prisons, legislation).

In the second half of the nineteenth century the safety of the highway was measured in terms of what was referred to colloquially as 'street violence'. This term related to any forms of criminal violence against the person which occurred in public places other than riots. Riotous gatherings were viewed more as a threat of violence against property than against the person. If street violence resulted in criminal proceedings the offences could range through robbery with violence, robbery, assault and battery, assault to commit grievous bodily harm (GBH) and assault to commit actual bodily harm (ABH). Thus, to understand the term 'street violence' the accepted legal parameters of such offences are best described.

The first statutory definition of robbery came with Section 8 (i) of the Theft Act 1968. Prior to this, problems of definition were resolved by recourse to the common law based on precendent. Using such precedent it was defined in 1854 as the felonious and forcible taking from the person of another, of goods or money to any value, by violence, or putting him in fear.[18] Robbery with wounding was robbery accompanied by an attempt to stab, cut or wound. If robbery was not proved a verdict of assault could be found. If larceny from the person was committed by two or more persons together it was treated as robbery with violence. If one person of a party was armed, others in the party who were aiding and abetting would be convicted of the same charge. When a defendant did not complete the act of assault against the person and was only found guilty of an attempt to commit the act he was still punished in the same manner as if the act had been committed.

It is apparent that robbery was differentiated from larceny from the person by the element of violence or putting in fear. Violence was deemed to be committed if personal injury was caused. The snatching of a diamond pin from a lady's hair, if part of the hair was torn away; running against a person to divert his attention while picking his pocket; hanging on to the prosecutor's person to deprive him of his power of resistance whilst rifling him of his watch although no actual force or menace was used; and a struggle for the possession of property, all constituted sufficient violence to elevate an action from being a larceny to being a robbery. Sudden snatching unawares did not constitute a robbery but snatching a watch causing the chain to break did. The fear required to justify the offence being termed a robbery had to be of such a nature as in reason and common experience to be likely to have induced a party to deliver up his property against his will. Such definitions are open to interpretation and it is easy to see how in times of public outrage many offences which would ordinarily have been classified as assault or larceny could become the serious offence of robbery. A button 'stolen' from a coat during a fight could make an assault into a robbery. A hair falling out whilst taking a hair-pin could turn simple larceny into a robbery if the police or magistrate wished to interpret it thus. Unfortunately for the defendant such nuances of interpretation could turn one month's imprisonment into fourteen years' penal servitude with hard labour.

These were the legal and administrative semantics of the media term 'street violence'. However, the media saw street violence as consisting of only three types. These were garotte robbery, brutal assault and ruffianism.

Garotte robbery or garotting is synonymous with the twentieth-century term 'mugging'. It referred at first to a specialised form of street violence and soon became an umbrella term covering all types of violent street robbery. The term garotte came from the Spanish instrument of execution, the garotta (thought, incidentally, to be the origin of the phrase 'It's an old Spanish custom'), which was publicised with the execution of General Lopez on 1 September 1851 at Havanna. Lopez had invaded Cuba and was hunted down with bloodhounds prior to his public garotting. 'Our newspapers described the process and naturalised the word'.[19] According to the *Illustrated Times* (3 January 1863), 'so great was the fascination of horror implied by the mode of death so described that the people took the earliest opportunity of adopting the word, and the verb 'to garotte' was found useful to denote a method of robbery with violence which arose at about the same time'. Until this time the newspapers referred to these types of robbery as acts of thuggee. The first use of the word in reference to a robbery was by James Brockbank of the Middle Temple in a letter to *The Times*, 12 February 1851. He had been attacked and strangled and was convinced that 'an application of this human garotte to an elderly person, or to anyone in a bad state of health, might very easily occasion death'. *The Annual Register* for 1862 summed up garotting as:

> a method of highway plunder, which consists in one ruffian seizing an unsuspecting traveller by the neck and crushing his throat, while another rifles his pockets; the scoundrels then decamp, leaving their victim on the ground writhing in agony, with tongue protruding and eyes starting from their sockets, unable to give an alarm or to attempt a pursuit.

The *Cornhill Magazine*[20] gave a less alarmist account of what it referred to as 'the science'. The attacker it referred to as the 'nasty man', accompanied by a 'back and front stall' (the latter being pickpocket cant). The article listed three different variations which may have been used in addition to the classic garotte which brought the forearm across the Adam's Apple, cutting off the air supply until the victim was unconscious. The first involved a 'nasty man' working alone from doorways. Secondly, a brutal or inexpert thief may have pressed his fingers into the throat. Lastly a stick may have been used for the garotte. The well-executed garotte was moderately harmless. It was believed that convicts learned the method of garotting from gaolers on convict ships who used the technique to control troublesome convicts. However, in 1857, small figures of Indian thugs engaged in thuggee were removed to a private room of the British Museum because the Chaplain of Newgate was convinced that the exhibit had suggested the practice of garotting to English thieves.[21]

It was the brutal variations which the newspapers educated their readers to fear. The first of these attacks was reported in a letter to *The Times*, 3 October 1850. 'Publico' wrote of an attack on his friend who was 'seized by three men and an instrument placed round his neck, by which he was completely throttled'. By January 1851, *The Times* was referring to the 'New System of Robbery' in Manchester and in

December 1851, under the heading 'The Garotte in Birmingham' noted the increase in 'garotte' robberies. The 'garotte' had arrived in the press and within a year was so familiar a term to newspaper readers that it had lost its inverted commas. By 1858 the garotter was so familiar a figure in the minds of the public that J. Ewing-Ritchie, describing a visit to a night-house off the Tottenham Court Road, could write that at two in the morning everyone in the neighbourhood was in bed 'with the exception of one or two amiable garotters, a few sleepy policemen and some three or four women'. On visiting Highbury Barn he observed 'a dark passage, admirably adapted for a garotte walk'.[22]

V

Many researchers into nineteenth-century crime lament the lack of research into the unresearchable without admitting the impossibility of such research. For example, Jennifer Davis has stated that, 'the question of how the lower classes perceived their own law-breaking activities is one that has been largely neglected by historians, and certainly merits research'.[23] Surely such a question is neglected precisely because it does not merit research for it is virtually unresearchable. The working of the minds of nineteenth-century criminals is lost to us forever. Even the minds of the honest section of the lower socio-economic groups are a source desert. Owing to a widespread illiteracy (amongst other grinding factors including lack of time, materials with which to write, and publishers) there are few nineteenth-century works comparable to that of Evelyn Haythorne[24] and the abundance of similar works on twentieth-century working-class life as portrayed by those who have actually experienced such a life. Thomas Wright,[25] the skilled artisan, was almost as close as we may come to reading the thoughts of the lower socio-economic groups. Working-class 'opinion' was expressed in broadsheets but these were usually written for political and commercial motives by lower-middle-class authors who wrote that which they believed the working classes wanted to read. Far more usual was the literary production of the middle-class explorer who ventured into the social depths and, on surfacing, reported to an astonished middle class his own perception of his discoveries.[25] Unfortunately there is no great wealth of literary evidence written by authors from the lower socio-economic groups waiting to be unearthed although it should be noted that E.P. Thompson believes that in the first half of the century the poor 'had discovered themselves and the Northern Star contained a part of their own testament'.[26]

Other researchers, refusing to admit defeat, have turned to other sources to understand the nineteenth-century criminal. Harvey Graff has urged the use of gaol registers of municipal prisons in the study of the Canadian Victorian criminal. However, he fails to state how they should be used and ducks the issue with the comment that methodological considerations, 'are largely questions for the individual historian'.[27] A similar source has been used by Monkkenen in his study of crime and poverty in late-Victorian Columbus, Ohio, in which he professes to 'examine quantitatively, those persons who formed what was known as the dangerous class. Thus, this is an exercise in history from the bottom up'.[28] The author laments that 'historians have rarely studied the criminal experience' and has attempted to do so by using published state statistics, unpublished statistics from the county court and poorhouse records and the lists of names of criminal defendants and paupers admitted to the poorhouse in conjunction with lists from the city directories and the 1870 manuscript census. This valuable research concludes that industrialisation and urbanisation did not create a dangerous class and that poverty caused by structural alterations during industrialisation did not lead to an increase in crime. Its primary conclusion is that the 'dangerous class is found to blend with the normal population, showing more differences of degree than kind'. All the sources on which this research was based were compiled by the middle-class control structure and the subject of the research – the dangerous class was itself a middle-class myth created to account for the potential social forces that they feared might disrupt their relatively comfortable lives.

If one takes a middle-class myth and then measures its reflection in sources compiled by the middle-class dominated control structure in society, it is not surprising that it will be analysed as a myth. If a social class blends in with the normal population it is not a social class. Far from being an 'exercise in history from the bottom up' such research is an exercise in history from the middle down and reflected back. As it is society that makes a criminal a criminal, there is little justification in research from the bottom up. To attempt to understand crime and its relevance to nineteenth-century society the researcher must approach, not from the bottom up, but from the middle down. 'Crime' as a cause or a result of social change was not a lower socio-economic group act but a middle-class perception of that act. Therefore, the interest lies not with the motivation of the lower-class act but with the foundation of the middle-class perception. In fact, the middle classes were capable of perceiving acts which may never have actually happened or suddenly perceiving acts which had been occurring unremarked for years. Roger

Lane, describing middle-class concerns about crime in nineteenth-century Massachusetts reported that although the concerns were very real they 'had little to do with the overall crime rate'.[29]

The present work admits the impossibility of understanding the nineteenth-century criminal and acknowledges that it is based on middle-class sources (i.e. statistics and newspaper reports) and as such can only analyse the middle-class perception of, and reaction to, street violence. It is these middle-class sources to which attention is turned in chapters two and three.

Notes

1. G.M. Young, *The Portrait of an Age: Victorian England* (1936) VI
2. A.F. Weber, *The Growth of Cities in the Nineteenth Century: A Study in Statistics* (New York, 1899).
3. 'A feeling very generally exists that the condition and disposition of the Working Classes is a rather ominous matter at present; that something ought to be said, something ought to be done, in regard to it'. T. Carlyle *Chartism* (1839) 3.
4. A.P. Stanley, *The Miscellaneous Works of Thomas Arnold* (1845) 453.
5. See D. Roberts, *Paternalism in Early Victorian England* (1979).
6. Ibid., 98.
7. H.J. Dyos, preface to A. Wohl, *The Eternal Slum: Housing and Social Policy in Victorian London*, (1977) VII.
8. See for example, D. Philips, *Crime and Authority in Victorian England: The Black Country 1835 –60*, (1977); J.J. Tobias, *Crime and Industrial Society in the Nineteenth Century* (1967); H. Zehr, *Crime and the Development of Modern Society: Patterns of Criminality in Nineteenth-Century Germany and France* (1976).
9. In 1982 the rate was 6,577 per 100,000. The rate per 100,000 population of robberies known to the police in England and Wales in 1862, a panic year, was 2.8 compared to 46 (174 in the Metropolitan Police District) in 1982. The total number of indictable offences in England and Wales on average for the three years 1857–60 was 51,457 compared to a 1982 figure of 3,262,400. *Criminal statistics: England and Wales*, c. 9048; M. Pratt, *Mugging as a Social Problem* (1980) 75; F.H. McClintock and E. Gibson, *Robbery in London* (1961) 123.
10. H. Mayhew, *London Labour and the London Poor*, vol. IV (1862) 234.
11. Letter from 'L', *The Times*, 13 December 1843.
12. 'Convicts and Transportation' *North British Review* LXXV (February 1863) 1–36.
13. *Liverpool Daily Post*, 4 September 1886.
14. Op.cit., *North British Review*.
15. T.B. Lloyd-Baker, *War with Crime* (1889) 20.

16. *Daily News*, 1 December 1862.
17. Gatrell, loc.sit.
18. See Leofric Temple, *A Synopsis of the Law Relating to Indictable Offences*, (2nd Edition, 1854).
19. *All the Year Round*, 4 February 1863.
20. 'The Science of Garotting and Housebreaking', *Cornhill Magazine*, 7, 1863 77–94.
21. Charlotte Lindgren, 'Nathaniel Hawthorne, Consul at Liverpool', *History Today*, 26, 8 August 1976, 516–524.
22. J. Ewing-Ritchie, *The Night Side of London* (1858) 154 and 163.
23. J. Davis, 'The London Garotting Panic of 1862: A Moral Panic and the Creation of a Criminal Class in mid-Victorian England', Gatrell, Lenman and Parker (eds), op.cit. (1980) 192.
24. E. Haythorne, *On Earth to make the Numbers Up* (1981).
25. Such an approach is evident in H. Mayhew, op.cit. (1862); T. Archer, *The Pauper, The Thief and the Convict* (1865); *The Terrible Sights of London* (1870); J. Greenwood, *The Seven Curses of London* (1869); *The Wilds of London* (1876); *The Policeman's Lantern* (1888).
26. E.P. Thompson, 'The Political Education of Henry Mayhew', *Victorian Studies*, IX, 1 September 1967, 43–62.
27. H.J. Graff, 'Crime and Punishment in the Nineteenth-Century: A New Look at the Criminal', *Journal of Interdisciplinary History* VII, 3, Winter 1977, 477–491.
28. E.H. Monkennen, *The Dangerous Class: Crime and Poverty in Columbus, Ohio, 1860–85* (1975) 2.
29. R. Lane, 'Urbanisation and Criminal Violence in the Nineteenth Century: Massachussets as a Test Case', in H. Davis Graham and T.R. Gurr, eds., *The History of Violence in America: Historical and Comparative Perspectives* (1969), 482.

2. A New Approach to Criminal Statistics

I

For those social historians whose main interest is the study of lower-class life the study of crime has become increasingly fashionable. However, the study of crime is the study of the whole of society and the relationship of the various classes within that society. That law-makers create law-breakers is axiomatic and the study of crime is, therefore, not just the study of criminals but also the institutions which defined them as criminals. For too long it has been implied that studying criminals is the study of a sub-set of lower-class life. This is a reflection of the fact that research is largely a middle-class occupation and so researchers bring to their work their own middle-class perception of society. The result is the automatic acceptance that crime consists purely of larceny, burglary, assault, rape and murder whilst overlooking the middle-class crimes of fraud, embezzlement, tax evasion, offences against the Companies Acts, Consumer Protection Acts and Factory Acts.

Monkkonen[1] has argued that the major focus of research should be towards the analysis and understanding of the criminal justice system, for the criminal is the product of the system and if a true understanding of the criminal is to be gained then it is the machinery that created the criminal which should be studied. Valuable work has been done on the role of the police in the criminal justice system notably by Storch, Miller, Emsley and Steedman[2] but the main thrust of research into crime in the nineteenth century has been based on analyses of criminal statistics. This chapter hopes to demonstrate the pitfalls of such an approach and offers an alternative and potentially more fruitful use to which such statistics may be put.

II

From 1810 the tables of the Assize Courts and Quarter Sessions in

England and Wales were annually presented to Parliament starting with those for 1805–9, listing fifty major offences in alphabetical order and the number of committals for each offence. Throughout the century one of the major limitations of the statistics was that they dealt with committals rather than crimes committed or criminals. Instances were known of one person committed a hundred times and amongst juveniles recommittals of ten times were not infrequent.[3] A parliamentary inquiry of 1847 was told that the 'criminal population is much smaller than is generally imagined' and an example was given of fourteen people with 'a constant habit of making and uttering false coin'. As the issue of each coin was a separate offence these fourteen people had committed an estimated 20,000 offences.[4] Another major limitation of the Home Office statistics at this time was that they did not record the large groups of offenders who were dealt with summarily by magistrates – a number estimated to be often four times greater than that of those indicted (i.e. dealt with by higher courts). Minor offences were treated summarily by a Justice of the Peace at the Petty Sessions. More serious offences were indicted before a Grand Jury and then sent for trial by jury at an Assize Court presided over by a circuit judge or at a Quarter Sessions chaired by a Justice of the Peace. The allocation of indictable cases between the Assizes and Quarter Sessions was governed, after 1848, by the convention that the Quarter Sessions tried all indictable offences except those carrying maximum sentences of life imprisonment on first conviction, and burglary. Non-indictable offences were generally in the nature of nuisances.

It was not until 1857 that the first comprehensive Judicial Statistics were published covering the year 1856. This resulted from the County and Borough Police Act 1856 and their collection was aided by the returns of the police forces created by the Act. These showed numbers of persons apprehended or proceeded against for both summary and indictable offences: the number of depredators, offenders and suspects at large; the size of the police establishment and charges; the number of crimes committed and the population for the police district at the last census. They were presented for each police district. In addition, the Judicial Statistics showed the personal characteristics (i.e. age, degree of instruction, etc.) of people imprisoned. These were presented on a county basis. Although vastly improved, the Judicial Statistics remained imperfect in several respects until a Departmental Committee was appointed in 1892 to reorganise the criminal section. The Committee created a basic uniformity which had previously been lacking, by stating the precise terms and definitions to be used and the statistics have remained largely unchanged in format since that date.

Hammick[4] discerned several shortcomings of the Judicial Statistics which appeared after 1857. These included the paucity of information that they revealed concerning judicial establishments, organisation of the legal system and the machinery by which justice was administered. For example, for all their power in summary courts, the number of magistrates in England and Wales remained unknown throughout most of the century. The tables also do not indicate whether the prisoner was tried at Assize Court or Quarter Sessions, make no mention of courts martial, and omitted the number of jurors at the trial. The number could be five or twelve but it was never known which worked more efficiently. This lack of information limits the possibility of assessing the different biases which must have inevitably existed between geographical areas, different types of court and between individual magistrates and judges. An example of the eccentricity of magistrates is afforded by T.J. Arnold, a magistrate for Hammersmith and Westminster from 1860-72 who dismissed all cases where the police inspector was not in attendance although the inspector was responsible for both courts and attended the one with the most cases.[6]

Until 1893 there was little uniformity of definition among those who contributed to the returns and this is one of the major limitations of the statistics if used for comparative purposes both over time and between geographical areas. Prior to 1863, in Gloucestershire, a 'known thief' was anyone who had ever been convicted of larceny. The Yorkshire authorities excluded anyone who was engaged in honest work at the time the return was made.[7] In 1890, the number of 'known thieves' under sixteen years of age was 192, while in Birmingham there were only 23 and in Manchester none. The total of 'thieves' and 'suspicious characters' was higher for the county of Stafford than that for the metropolis. It is unlikely that these figures reflect real comparison between the number of thieves in such areas. Rather they are merely evidence of the problems of definition which were tackled locally in different ways.

The police were instructed by the Home Office to enter in the returns only those cases which, in their opinion, if discovered, would have been classified as an indictable offence. The constantly changing scope of summary jurisdiction in the middle decades of the century made such a forecast a matter of debate for a lawyer and was certainly not a subject on which a policeman was likely to be consistently correct. In 1866 the Recorder of Birmingham remarked that: 'Crime in Sheffield, Leeds and Birmingham was taken to hve a very different meaning from what it had in the minds of those who made the returns for Liverpool and Manchester.'[8] A stipendiary magistrate replied that he found, 'in

Manchester many crimes and offences were included in the returns which in other places would have been excluded altogether, and that, in fact, the statistics were useless for comparison'.[9] The Chief Constable of Manchester concluded that police officers had differing views so that 'without some definite rule to guide them' he believed that 'any information founded on such returns cannot be considered trustworthy.'[10]

Problems of definition caused a large disparity between the number of murders returned by the police and the returns of the coroner's inquests. This was a result of the police not defining infanticide as murder but as 'concealment of birth'. Hence, in 1865 the total number of murders in England and Wales returned by the police as 135, while coroner's inquests returned 227 cases. Similarly, there is not the expected uniformity between police returns of non-indictable offenders and prison returns for the same category. Prison returns were invariably higher as police returns were based on the numbers sentenced while prison returns included those automatically imprisoned for non-payment of fines. In 1850 the criminal statistics showed 70,000 sentenced to imprisonment but 127,000 committed to prison. According to W.L. Clay[11] the 57,000 discrepancy included some 15,000 who spent a few days in prison while on remand or awaiting sureties, 5,000 military offenders tried by courts martial and 22,000 imprisoned for safe custody or pending payment of fines.

That the primary source for such statistics, the criminal, is dishonest and so unreliable as a source is a fundamental weakness of all criminal statistics. It was often advantageous to lie about one's age and identity. A juvenile offender may have given an older age in order to be sent to prison for a short period of time rather than to a reformatory for at least two years.[12] No central records were kept of offenders until the introduction of the Register of Habitual Criminals[13] in 1869 so that it was possible to run the round of local police offices and always be treated as a first offender. The criminals would also exploit weaknesses in the law. For some indictable offences[14] a plea of guilty meant that the case was dealt with summarily. This would normally not only result in a lighter sentence but, unfortunately for the social historian, turned such offenders into statistical nonentities as police returns did not show indictable offences treated summarily. This resulted in the ratio of crimes committed to criminals apprehended being misrepresented. In 1890, for example, 35,306 persons were charged with larceny but dealt with summarily.

Comparison of different returns is made more hazardous by the fact that such returns were often collected on different dates and therefore annual returns appertain to different twelve-month periods. Until 1892 (when the statistical year was officially that ending on 31 December) the police returns were submitted on 27 September, the Quarter Sessions and Assize Courts on 31 December, Local and Convict Prison returns on 31 March, Reformatory and Industrial Schools on 29 September and returns from criminal lunatics on 31 October. A similar problem of dating occurs in the police returns of 'tramps and beggars'. In 1863 the daily average was based on the numbers who spent the night in a given district on one stated night in September. In 1865 the number was ascertained for a night in April. Such a change would cause an apparent geographical shift of vagrants as such people tended to migrate to rural areas in the spring during the time of good weather and when casual work was plentiful, while spending the autumn and winter in the warmth of the towns and cities when the impersonality of the poor relief system made such relief more obtainable. Other changes affected the police returns more than the other available records. From 1867 to 1893 only larcenies where goods worth more than five shillings were involved or an arrest took place were recorded. Prior to 1861 the Metropolitan Police returns for 'known thieves' included anyone who had ever been convicted. After 1861 those who were no longer thought to be active criminals were excluded and after 1864 those who had not committed a crime for at least one year were omitted.

Method of definition, collection and presentation, therefore, made the statistics unreliable as evidence in certain cases. Even if such unreliability can be countered the use of these statistics for discerning trends in criminality over time still lacks validity as several factors were constantly at work causing distortions in the figures. Throughout the century there were changes in the law, changes in police effectiveness and changes in the spirit with which the law was administered, all of which would produce an apparent change in the number of 'criminals' or the amount of 'criminality' in a given area. If a 'criminal' is defined as a person who contravenes the criminal law, then changes in the law effectively change the meaning of the term 'criminal'. Changes also occurred in the administrative procedure following the contravention of the law. The most important example of this was the varying jurisdiction of the magistrate as defined by the various Summary Jurisdiction Acts throughout the century. Comparison of pre-1879 and post-1879 statistics must be treated with extreme caution, especially if statistics for indictable and non-indictable offences are not used in conjunction with each other, as the Summary Jurisdiction Act 1879 had the immediate effect of transferring 3,000 cases formerly classified as indictable to summary courts.

Between 1848 and 1850 the number of juvenile offenders rose as the age of maturity was raised from fourteen to sixteen years. A similar change occurred in the category of sexual offences. Prior to 1875, sexual intercourse with a person under the age of ten years was a felony but with a person between the ages of ten and twelve years was only classified as a misdemeanour. Amidst great opposition the age of consent was raised to thirteen years in 1875 and to sixteen years in 1885.

It would be impossible to compile a detailed list of every change in the criminal law in the nineteenth century or to make an estimate of the impact on criminal activity due to legislative change. It should be recalled that much of the social legislation of the second half of the century led to convictions. For example, the Elementary Education Act led to over 500,000 cases between 1870 and 1892.[15] Inability to pay the poor rate could lead to the imprisonment of the householder and prosecutions were common under a wide variety of public health legislation. Such prosecutions would usually result in a fine or an order and so would be unrecorded, but failure to pay a fine or obey an order would mean the case being transferred to a higher court and would automatically lead to imprisonment.

Throughout the century the effectiveness of the police in bringing guilty parties to court and securing a conviction did improve. In 1858 40 per cent of those brought before metropolitan magistrates were discharged, reflecting the lack of police thoroughness in collecting evidence. By 1861 this number had fallen to 33 per cent and by 1865 was down to 30 per cent.[16] Police effectiveness and standards were constantly improving throughout the period although there has been little research into the spirit with which they carried out their duties and how they decided on which types of crime to focus their increasing efficiency. The formation of the Thames River Police in 1800, the Horse Patrol in 1805, the Metropolitan Police in 1829, the passing of the permissive Rural Police Act of 1839, the formation of the Metropolitan Detective Office in 1842, the creation of police forces throughout the country by the County and Borough Police Act of 1856, and the establishment of a separate Criminal Investigation Department in 1878 all marked a widening of the power and an increase in the effectiveness of the law enforcement agencies. It is one of the ironies of the subject that an increasingly efficient police force produces, on paper, an increasing number of criminals.

In all periods of history there are changes in the spirit with which the law is administered and during certain periods greater degrees of emphasis are put on the seriousness of certain offences. During 1846 and 1847 the government paid great attention to the operation of the Game

Laws and magistrates were required to submit reports on all convictions to the Home Secretary. This would have tended to focus the attention of magistrates on such cases and may be a major factor in accounting for the large increase in the number of prosecutions under these laws in three years. A similar focus was put on burglary in the 1850s, robbery with violence in the 1860s and brutal assaults in the 1870s.

The introduction of Reformatory Schools in 1854, of which forty had been built by 1860, gave magistrates an alternative form of punishment to imprisonment for juveniles. This would have made juries more willing to convict. The creation of Parkhurst as a reception prison for juvenile offenders sentenced to transportation would have increased the number of juvenile offenders given this sentence as the magistrature knew that, in reality, such a sentence meant a permanent stay in the reception prison. Thus many sentences of transportation appeared to be more serious than they were in reality.

It is apparent that the usefulness of the judicial statistics is seriously limited by the lack of uniformity in the methods of their collection and the reflection by the statistics of factors extraneous to the actual numbers of crimes committed. These factors are related to the historical situation but there are several additional factors which ensure that the major part of the true picture of the state of crime will always be obscured. These factors include the amount of hidden crime, the amount of unsolved crime, the differences in enforcement of the law between districts and the allied phenomenon of biased prosecution.

Hidden crime or the 'dark number' refers to those crimes that are committed but of which the authorities are not notified and therefore they go unrecorded. Such an amount defies exact quantification and despite the claims of those who base their research on criminal statistics, there is no justification of why the figure should be a stable proportion of the total crime picture. To give an idea of the size of the problem Jones made an educated guess putting the dark number at about four times the number of crimes known to the police. Given that about 30 per cent of the latter figure are successfully prosecuted this means that it is possible that only 8 per cent of crime ends in a court sentence.[17] As such a large amount of crime goes unsolved, even if not hidden, the numbers of criminals involved remains unknown, so that ten robberies may have been the work of either one man or of ten separate gangs with four or five members each.

On the subject of the enforcement of the law and the related question of biased prosecutions, Clay remarked in 1857 that in areas where crime was rare it was fully punished and vice versa. The law was certainly not enforced to the same degree in different counties for the 'want of uniformity in administering the law is very apparent.'[18] As in the present century there is evidence that the forces of the law were biased against the lower socio-economic groups. According to Mary Carpenter, writing in 1853, the children of the upper classes were given stern warnings by adults for petty thefts for which members of the lower classes would be subject 'to imprisonment, even to transportation, a prison brand being affixed for life to the unfortunate children', and that 'whatever moral delinquency exists in the higher and middle classes of society, the avenging hand of the law falls almost exclusively on the lower.'[19]

III

It is apparent from the evidence that as a direct measure of criminality the usefulness of the criminal statistics is highly suspect. Andreski has noted that, 'there is no reason whatsoever to presume that amenability to measurement must correspond to importance',[20] and that it is partial realisation of this that has led recent writers on crime whose research is based on the criminal statistics to commit literary contortions in attempting to link their opening remarks on the unreliability of the statistics with the main body of their work, which is based upon them. Baroness Wootton has written:

> That we should reject the official statistics as evidence of criminal trends is a hard doctrine, because it means that we must be content to confess ourselves quite ignorant as to whether our population is becoming more, or less, addicted to crime. Nevertheless, such ignorance has to be admitted.[21]

It is indeed a hard doctrine, given such a wealth of criminal statistics, to know that they are so riddled with pitfalls and inconsistencies that as a measure of the state of crime they may be useless. The debate centres on whether the pitfalls render the statistics useless or merely imperfect. In his chapter entitled 'Quantification as Camouflage', Andreski puts such a debate into perspective.

> As has often been said, measurement is the beginning of science (if we mean thereby exact science) because our ability to predict the behaviour of a phenomenon must remain very restricted until we can measure it. It does not follow, however, that no knowledge whatsoever is possible without measurement, nor that such knowledge cannot be worth having ... But the true scientific spirit consists of trying to obtain the nearest approximation to

truth which is possible under the circumstances and it is puerile to demand perfect exactitude or nothing.[22]

Tobias claims that, 'The criminal statistics have little to tell us about crime and criminals in the nineteenth century' and 'when they point to a conclusion opposed to that based on contemporary description they can perhaps be disregarded without much anxiety'.[23] This view is supported by the Royal Statistical Society as being 'amply borne out'.[24] Other writers have argued that much of the contemporary description was based on the criminal statistics and so Tobias's statement is invalid.[25] Andreski rightly argues that to demand 'perfect exactitude or nothing' is puerile but later speaks against the 'soul destroying taboo against touching anything that cannot be quantified.[26] The question seems to be whether there is an alternative method to the truth about the state of crime in the nineteenth century other than the inexactitude of the criminal statistics. Tobias would answer that literary sources supply such a route but it seems that many literary sources are either reworkings of the criminal statistics or rewrites of received myths and as such are a poor substitute. We are left with a Nietzchean feeling that rather than admitting to knowing nothing about the state of crime in the nineteenth century we have to substitute a truth created from dubious statistics, so that 'these people know with perfect accuracy a past that has never existed'.[27] This is evident in several recent works based on criminal statistics.

Gatrell and Hadden, in their paper on criminal statistics purport to 'explain the structure of the nineteenth century returns and to discuss the difficulties and dangers in utilising them, showing how they may be circumvented' and assure the reader that 'none of these deficiencies ... seriously impedes the sensitive exploitation of returns', although concluding that, 'Two deficiencies cannot be circumvented: the fact that they can never reflect the "actual" extent of criminal behaviour in society, and the fact that legal and police developments must affect the consistency of the relationship between this unknowable figure and the recorded incidence of reported criminal activity across a period of time'.[28] To admit to such a deficiency and then proceed on the basis that the admission has neutralised its own negative import is pointless. In a later paper Gatrell again admits that we shall never know the relationship between recorded and actual crime and that crime rates tell us nothing about how much crime is committed in society. He even states that 'the less conventionally serious and the more numerous the offences, the greater the effect on its levels of report and prosecution of changing public, police and judicial attitudes,[29] and then produces a paper arguing the decline of theft between 1834 and 1914, based on the statistics.

Howard Zehr admits that 'crime statistics, like most statistical indexes offer innumerable possibilities of misinterpretation and misuse', but assures us that, 'a close study of various crime indexes from both the nineteenth and twentieth centuries indicates that nineteenth-century criminal statistics are more powerful and provide better indexes of delinquent behaviour than is commonly assumed'. Zehr, however, offers no basis for this assurance and, as such, it would seem to fall into the category of things people want to believe. Similarly he states that: 'Records from the nineteenth century yield recurrent and comprehensible patterns of crime which cannot be attributed simply to biases in the records or to the activities of the agencies who compiled them'.[30] Again, Zehr does not back up his statement with evidence and until a statistical model is constructed which can demonstrably quantify and neutralise such bias it seems that such statements are acts of faith rather than of fact. The weakness of criminal statistics are also admitted by David Philips.[31] He cites Cicourel and Kitsuse who have suggested that the official crime rates, though imperfect for studying the 'total crime' picture, are useful precisely because of their imperfection, since they represent the end result of the process of interaction between the authorities and the law-breakers, and can be used to give us a picture of that process in action.[32] In fact crime rates do not show the process in action, merely the result of the process in action. They give us no insight into the mechanisms and relationships involved in the process at all. In addition to the 'dark number', McClintock and Avison note three limitations which are built into the criminal statistics that they use to describe the state of crime in England and Wales in the present century. Firstly, they acknowledge that the basic units are based on legal definitions which give an inadequate indication of the nature of the offence. Secondly, that the police and Home Office treat 'crime' as being synonymous with 'indictable offences'. Finally, they note that the number of people being dealt with by the courts is affected by changes in the criminal law or criminal procedure. The authors, however, conclude that the official returns, 'if judicially interpreted' will 'yield much information that is of considerable value' and lead to 'furthering our knowledge of the state of crime'.[33] Michael Pratt admits that 'no one is likely to suggest that the published crime statistics indicate in any way the "true" amount of crime (however defined) that has occurred – neither can the indicated rate be thought of as a sample, since the whole cannot be specified'. He then writes:

The best that can be done is to take note of the fact that the figures do not reflect the true position, and hope that, at least as far as the serious crime of robbery is concerned, that this will not affect too critically any comparisons that may be made.[34]

Thus a formula seems to have been developed amongst criminologists and criminal historians which involves the acknowledgement of the facts which make impossible the gaining of a true picture of the state of crime through the analysis of statistics. This is followed by wise pronouncements concerning 'judicious interpretation', 'taking bias into account', 'acknowledging imperfections', prior to analysis of the statistics to produce a picture of the state of crime – whether true or not. This somewhat depressing state of affairs seems, at first, to confront the researcher into nineteenth-century crime with a dilemma. He can, as Tobias has done, consign the criminal statistics to the waste-paper bin, or he can, as Gatrell, Zehr and Philips have done, use them to produce an image of crime which is comfortingly based on numbers and allow the fact that the numbers are almost irrelevant to the true state of crime to fade into the background.

There is, however, a third approach. This is to view the statistics not as a reflection of a phenomenon but as a phenomenon in themselves. It was on the criminal statistics, not the actual state of crime, that both individuals and institutions based their beliefs about the actual state of crime. Thus to look at the criminal statistics is to look at the statistics that the Victorians themselves used to gauge the state of crime in their society. There is no dispute that viewed from this perspective the criminal statistics are real enough. As the cause of certain reactions, such as self-protection, increased policing and new legislation, they are immensely useful in explaining the reactions themselves. The statistics are therefore a measure, not necessarily of what was happening, but of what people believed was happening. Such statistics were debated in Parliament and reported in the press. It was through the knowledge of such statistics, rather than the observation of criminal acts themselves, that Victorians could conclude in the 1840s that, 'the progress of wickedness is so much more rapid than the increase of the numbers of people',[35] and in the 1890s that, 'we have witnessed ... a decline in the spirit of lawlessness'.[36] Their value lies in forming the basis of the picture of crime which powerful influences in nineteenth-century society thought confronted them. They were as influential in the nineteenth-century as television pictures of isolated incidents are in the twentieth in creating an image of that unseen but threatening world that surrounds every individual.

Notes

1. E. Monkkonen, 'The Quantitative Historical Study of Crime and Criminal Justice' in J.A. Inciardi and C.E. Faupel, (eds), *History and Crime: Implications for Criminal Justice Policy* (1980).
2. R.D. Storch, 'The plague of blue locusts: Police reform and popular resistance in northern England, 1840-57, *International Rev. Social History*, XXX (1975); Miller, 'The policeman as domestic missionary: urban discipline and popular culture in northern England, 1850-80', *Social History* IX, 4 (1976); C. Emsley, *Policing and its Context, 1750-1870* (1983); C. Steedman, *Policing the Victorian Community: The Formation of English Provincial Police Forces, 1856-80* (1984).
3. M. Carpenter, *Reformatory Schools* (19851) 4-5.
4. Evidence of F. Hill, Prisoner Inspector, to Select Committee of House of Lords on the Criminal Law.
5. J.T. Hammick, *Statistical Soc.* XXX (1867), 375-425.
6. Letter from Wandsworth Division to the Police Commissioner, 10 Aug. 1863. P-R-O MePo 3/35.
7. T.B. Lloyd-Baker, *Statistical Soc.* XXIII (1860), 427.
8. Reported in *J. of Statistical Soc.* XXXI (Sept. 1865), 350.
9. R. Fowler, letter to *Manchester Guardian*, 12 Feb. 1866.
10. *Criminal and Miscellaneous Statistical Returns of the Manchester Police for year ended 29th September 1866*, Manchester Local History Library 352.2.ML.
11. W.L. Clay, *Prison Chaplain* (1861).
12. Under the Youthful Offenders Act of 1854 magistrates were empowered to send children under sixteen years of age to a reformatory for a period of between two and five years.
13. Set up by the Habitual Criminals Act of 1869 which was annulled and partially re-enacted by the Prevention of Crimes Act of 1871. The Register showed offence, sentence, name and aliases.
14. For example, larceny of goods worth more than five shillings following the Criminal Justice Act of 1855.
15. W.D. Morrison, 'The increase of Crime', *Nineteenth Century, XXXI* (1892), 950-7.
16. Hammick, op.cit., 394.
17. H. Jones, *Crime in a Changing Society* (1971), 18.
18. J. Clay, 'On the relationship between crime, popular instruction, attendance on religious worship and beer-houses', *Statistical Soc. XX* (1857), 22.
19. M. Carpenter, *Juvenile Delinquents* (1853).
20. S. Andreski, *Social Science as Sorcery* (1972), 142.
21. B. Wootton, *Social Science and Social Pathology* (1959), 25.
22. Andreski, op.cit, 123.
23. J.J. Tobias, *Crime and Industrial Society* (1967), 21, 255.
24. Private correspondence, Royal Statistical Soc. to author, 24 Sept. 1981.

25. For example, H. Zehr, *Crime and the Development of Modern Society: Patterns of Criminality in Nineteenth-Century Germany and France* (1976); D. Philips, *Crime and Authority in Victorian England: The Black Country 1835–60* (1977).
26. Andreski, op.cit., 136.
27. R.M. Rilke, *Mault Laurids Brigge*, trans. J.B. Leisham (1950).
28. V.A.C. Gatrell and T.B. Hadden, 'Criminal statistics and their interpretation', in E.A. Wrigley (ed.), *Nineteenth-Century Society: Essays in the Use of Quantitative Methods for the Study of Social Data* (1972), 339, 340, 361.
29. V.A.C. Gatrell, 'Theft and violence in England, 1834–1914', in V.A.C. Gatrell, B. Lenman and G. Parker (eds.) *Crime and the Law: A Social History of Crime in Western Europe since 1500* (1980), 240, 243, 248.
30. Zehr, op.cit., 14, 15.
31. Philips, op.cit., 45.
32. A. Cicourel and J.I. Kitsuse, 'A note on the uses of official statistics', *Social Problems, II* (autumn 1963) 131–9.
33. F.H. McClintock and N. Avison, *Crime in England and Wales* (1968), 6–12.
34. M. Pratt, *Mugging as a Social Problem* (1980), 69, 71.
35. 'Causes of the increase of crime', *Blackwoods Edinburgh Magazine LVI* (1844).
36. *Criminal Registrar's Report* (1899), 36–7.

3. *The Role of the Press*

I

Criminal statistics were one medium from which Victorians formulated a picture of the crime which surrounded them but which they rarely encountered. The newspaper press was the second such medium, and far more important in its influence, as it was responsible for both reporting criminal acts and disseminating criminal statistics. In order to estimate the usefulness of newspapers as primary sources in any form of research into social history it is useful to identify the role of the press in the society with which the social historian is concerned. Such identification requires the use of the analytical models offered by sociologists. Any historian interested in the role of the press in his particular period of history will find the model of Folk Devils and Moral Panics outlined by Stanley Cohen (1972)[1] a useful analytical tool.

Cohen's model is based on the activities of 'mods' and 'rockers' on holiday beaches in Britain in the mid-60s, but the reporting of street violence in the nineteenth century seems to fit the model, thus giving the model itself greater currency and helping the social historian better to understand the role of the press in Victorian society. Cohen explains his model as follows:

> Societies appear to be subject, every now and then, to periods of moral panic. A condition, episode, person or groups of persons emerges to become defined as a threat to societal values and interests; its nature is presented in stylised and stereotypical fashion by the mass media; the moral barricades are manned by editors, bishops, politicians and other right-thinking people; socially accredited experts pronounce their diagnosis and solutions; ways of coping are evolved or (more often) resorted to; the condition then disappears, submerges or deteriorates and becomes more visible. Sometimes the object of the panic is quite novel and at other times it is something which has been in existence long enough, but suddenly appears in the limelight. Sometimes the panic passes over and is forgotten, except in folk-lore and

collective memory: at other times it has more serious and long-lasting repercussions and might produce such changes as those in legal and social policy or even in the way society conceives itself.'[2]

It is the contention of this study that street violence in the nineteenth-century had been 'in existence long enough', although was probably on the increase, but was used as the object to create sporadic moral panics throughout the second half of the nineteenth century in which garotters and cornermen were conceived as the folk devils. The effect of these moral panics are studied in following chapters.

II

It was during the second half of the nineteenth century that the most dramatic growth in newspaper circulation occurred. The abolition of advertisement tax in 1853 and of stamp duty in 1855 removed the financial restraints on publication. At the same time technical improvements in printing presses allowed the hourly production rate of newspapers to rise from 4,000 in 1827 to 20,000 in 1847 and 168,000 after 1870.[3] This was accompanied by a fall in the price of paper per ream from 55 shillings in 1845 to 40 shillings in 1855. This trend was accelerated by the abolition of paper duty in 1860. The technical improvements in the transport and communications sectors during the century allowed the distribution by railway and, by 1871, the sale-or return distribution to railway bookstalls. From 1847 the electric telegraph was used for news collection although it was not fully exploited until the 1870s. All these innovations meant that by 1860 most daily newspapers sold for a penny and it is not surprising that between 1855 and 1860 the circulation of daily newspapers trebled and then doubled again between 1860 an 1870.

In addition to the dailies, the abolition of paper duty allowed a range of Sunday papers to break through into mass circulation. These included the *News of the World* (founded by John Brown Bell in 1843), the *Weekly Times* (founded by George Stiff in 1847), *Lloyd's Weekly Newspaper* (founded 1842) and *Reynolds' Newspaper* (founded by G.W.M. Reynolds in 1850). In 1850 total circulation of Sunday newspapers was 275,000 rising to 450,000 in 1855 and 1,725,000 in 1890. By 1890 *Lloyd's Weekly Newspaper*, aided by the vast public interest in the 'Jack the Ripper' murders (1889) had a circulation of 900,000.[4] The 'Sundays' were designed for the lower-middle and working classes. They were bought by institutions where they were publicly read. Many coffee houses offered a choice of up to one hundred dailies, weeklies and periodicals for an admission price of one penny. They were also collectively bought and read aloud in workshops but the barber's shop and the public house were increasingly the main reading places where people could read the week's news on their one free day, making full use of the advantages afforded by gas-light.[5]

By the 1850s the heyday of the quarterlies (such as the *Edinburgh Review*, *Quarterly Review* and *Westminster Review*) was past and they were soon eclipsed by the new progressive monthlies which reached the height of their influence between 1865 and 1914. These included the *Fortnightly Review* (founded in 1865 and turned monthly in 1866), the *Contemporary Review* (founded in 1866) and *Nineteenth Century* (founded in 1877).

Provincial newspapers were rarely a powerful influence in the first half of the century. Proprietors were primarily printers and only secondarily journalists and the content of the paper was rarely original. Most news or comment was lifted from the London press. In 1815 anti-Corn Law rallies in Manchester were not reported in the Manchester press and the resolutions passed at meetings had to be placed as advertisements in the local papers to achieve publicity. They did not try to influence local opinion and were either non-political or quietly supportive of existing local and national institutions. This changed with the growth of provincial, middle-class reform papers which acted as a 'platform from which the discontented could attack the authorities'.[6]

Throughout the century the content of the newspapers and the public that they supplied were gradually changing but it was from 1855 that the 'new journalism' – 'an attention to crime, sexual violence and human oddities' in contrast to dry political commentary – took over.[7] This was a journalism whose newness was marked by its commercialism. It was a press more interested in profit than political influence. The size of its readership gave it influence even if this was not its primary aim. George Newnes, one of the first of the new publishers, wrote to W.T. Stead of the *Pall Mall Gazette*, 'There is one kind of journalism which makes and unmakes Cabinets, upsets Governments, builds navies and does many other great things. That is your journalism. There is another kind which has no such great ambitions. That is my journalism. A journalism that pays'.[8] Burnham, in his history of the *Daily Telegraph* writes that, 'reviewing the files, the honest biographer cannot dispute that the *Daily Telegraph* thrived on crime'.[9] A survey of *Lloyd's Weekly News* for 1866 reveals that 50 per cent of its contents dealt with murder, crime and other thrilling events and its advertising emphasised its coverage of fire, robbery and murder.[10] It is interesting to note that sociological research has concluded from various 'reading and noting' studies that crime items are among those that carry a high 'thorough readership' score and that newspapers give a distorted impression of the relative frequency of different types of crime by over-representing more serious offences (i.e. crimes against the person, robbery, fraud, blackmail and drugs) so that there is no relationship between the quantity of crime news and the amount of crime reflected in the official crime statistics.[11] Both these factors are implicit in Cohen's Folk Devils model and there seems to be no reason why they should not have been equally valid in the second half of the nineteenth century as in the twentieth.

The 'new journalism' provided the lower but rising middle-class with news and diversity of opinion which readers of *The Times* might find lively, crude and vulgar but which required respectable newspapers (e.g. the *Morning Post* under Borthwick, 1852 – 1908) to publish very full reports of crimes. Writing in 1886, W.T. Stead warned that 'sensationalism is solely a means to an end. It is never an end in itself'. Such an end may have often been simply increased sales but it may also have been connected with the newspapers' influence on the affairs of society. Stead remarked that, 'nothing can ever get itself accomplished nowadays without sensationalism ... In politics, in social reform, it is indispensable' and proceeded to note that it was sensationalism that led to the appointment of the Royal Commission on Housing of the Poor and the passing of the Criminal Law Amendment Act in the 1880s.[12]

Under the influence of the telegraph the style of the 'new journalism' differed from the old and began more clearly to reflect the newspaper of the present day with a gain in simplicity and lack of padding, the use of shorter sentences, the over-simplification of complicated issues and the greater distortion caused by increasing use of the emphatic key word.

Only by the middle of the nineteenth century had the medium for the creation of folk devils and moral panics in the minds of the influential sector of public opinion (i.e. the middle classes) been developed to allow the creation of the garotters as the first folk devils and for their reported activities to allow a display of moral entrepreneurship in 1856[13] and the creation of the first moral panic in 1862. Newspapers had become the major medium in the dissemination of news and, more importantly, of opinion and so were in a position to be the prime movers in the development of moral panics.

III

Cohen's flow model has the following structure:-

1. *Initial deviance* eg leading to,
2. the *Inventory* and 3. *Sensitisation*, which feed back on each other and produce,
4. an *over-estimation* of the deviance which leads to,
5. an *escalation in the control culture.*

The initial deviance will be studied in the next chapter. It may be seen as acts of deviance which provoked the media to turn their attention to a phenomenon which had long been in existence.

The inventory refers to the process by which people first form a picture of what is happening. The power of the media lies in the fact that they make the public indirect witness to events of which it has no first hand experience. Individuals receive information about events from either personal experience or from the news. Where there is no common ground between the two sources of information there is a tendency to adopt the news as personal experience. As more selective living became possible the majority of the middle and upper classes, living in separate residential areas, had increasingly less direct knowledge of the lower socio-economic classes in general and of criminals in particular. In the traditional, predominantly rural society, the squirearchy had direct experience of the landless labourer, the poacher and the village idiot, but in the nineteenth century the process of urbanisation led to a trend towards segregation in which the wealthier classes moved outwards and lost direct contact with the poor. This direct contact was replaced by indirect experience through the medium of the press. In 1851 a parliamentary select committee was told that 'newspapers are the only thing that people will ever read' and 'all the information they get is through that means and conversation, all of which originated in the newspapers'.[14]

The typical inventory contains elements of exaggeration and distortion, prediction and symbolisation. The exaggeration and distortion are created largely by the mode and presentation of the information. The use of melodramatic vocabulary and the heightening of those elements in the story which are considered news; the use of the generic plural (e.g. a man being attacked becomes 'people were attacked'); and the reporting of the same incident twice so that it appears as two separate incidents are all methods of exaggeration and distortion used by the press which are noted by Cohen. The press will use the evidence of one reported incident as the basis for making implicit or explicit pessimistic predictions that the problem will recur or has become a permanent feature of society. By the use of key words and constant highlighting of certain aspects the press may initiate a process of symbolisation which educates the reader to make automatic assumptions concerning certain symbols e.g. occupation, dress, area of residence. Hence, in the 1850s, the term 'ticket-of-leave man' although actually meaning a convict pardoned for good behaviour on a ticket-of-leave became a symbol in the public mind which implied an active, violent, unfeeling criminal. Symbolisation involves three processes. A word becomes symbolic of deviant status and objects or actions symbolise the word. Eventually the objects or actions symbolise the deviant status. In 1874 the word 'cornerman' symbolised the type of deviant who was reported to have kicked Richard Morgan to death. The factory operative's boot became the symbol of cornermen and eventually if anyone was reported as wearing boots the implication was that they were of brutal ruffian status.

The third aspect of Cohen's model is sensitisation. This is the increased awareness in the reader of items of a similar nature which he might otherwise have ignored if it were not for the folk devil image which the inventory had created. The effects of sensitisation are:

1. greater notice being taken of signs of the deviance occurring;
2. a reclassification of events in terms of folk devils, e.g. by 1863 any form of theft in the street accompanied by any violence (even jostling) was referred to by the press as a garotte attack;
3. a crystallisation of the symbolisation process.

Symptoms of sensitisation are both a product of, and help to intensify, the moral panic. A classic example of such symptoms (referred to in more detail later) was the number of 'garotte' attacks which, in fact, were instances of mutually distrustful commuters attacking the person following them in the fog, believing that they were pre-empting a garotte attack. Such incidents, which provided *Punch* with a great source of amusement, were reported as garotte incidents and so fuelled the fires of panic.

The inventory and sensitisation processes are mutually heightening which results in an over-estimation of the deviance. It is then that moral entrepreneurs exploit the situation to bring about an increase in the control culture. A successful 'moral entrepreneur' has two pre-requisites. There must be a pyramidal conception of responsibility and blame and a parallel belief system which views the phenomenon as being only the visible tip of a more broadly-based condition. Both these conditions were present in the nineteenth century and have been analysed in greater detail in other chapters. The pyramidal conception of responsibility and blame started with the police and the philanth-ropists and worked up through the judiciary and the Director of Prisons to the Home Secretary and so on to the legislature.

The garotters, cornermen, Trafalgar Square rioters and the High Rip gang were seen as the visible tip of the 'dangerous classes' – a spectre which had haunted the middle and ruling classes since the French revolution. Food riots, rick-burning, Luddism, Chartism, election riots, political demonstrations, ruffianism and criminal violence were all viewed as tangible proof of the existence of the 'dangerous classes' and the need to control them if the revolutionary turmoil of 1848 which Britain's European neighbours had undergone was not to sweep through the country. As an industrial dispute resulting in strike action in twentieth-century Britain is viewed by many as the visible tip of Marxist infiltration, then a garotte in the nineteenth century was the proof of the latent power of the 'dangerous classes'.

Whilst attacking the folk devils and exploiting the moral panic, the moral entrepreneurs (that is, the newspapers) create folk heroes in the form of brave policemen or hardline magistrates and judges who fight the devil single-handed. Anthony Smith has written on the press in the 1840s and 1850s as 'setting itself up to act as a "moral gendarmerie" – a corrupt and licentious would-be censor of vice'.[155] Part of the process involves the setting of 'examples' as a warning to other 'devils' that they would not triumph over right-thinking society. The nineteenth century produced few hero policemen. Some of the judiciary did adopt the mantle of folk heroes. Baron Bramwell, presiding over the November sessions of the Central Criminal Court in 1862 handed down sentences designed to 'terrorise'[16] the criminal fraternity. According to William Bent the garotting outbreak in Manchester 1865–66 was crushed 'by the courageous hand of a strong administrator to bring its [the law's] effect into play. That hand was found in Mr Justice Lush'.[17] In 1874 the murderers of Richard Morgan were sentenced to be hanged although the Home Secretary had to consider the jury's recommendation of mercy for one of the defendants. *The Times* pronounced that, 'the occasion calls imperatively for stern justice, and can be satisfied with nothing less. The Judge and jury have done their duty, and we refuse to believe that the Home Secretary will be found wanting'.[18] The judge had been awarded folk-hero status but the Home Secretary's receipt of the title was in the balance.

These folk heroes handed out exemplary sentences to those unlucky enough to have their deviant act coincide with a moral panic. In November 1861 one person appeared before the Central Criminal Court charged with robbery with violence, having previous convictions. He was sentenced to one year in the House of Correction. In November 1862 two people were charged with the offence, also having previous convictions. They received sentences of life and twenty years penal servitude.[19] Tony Parker researched the case of a Teddy boy in the 1950s who stabbed another youth. He was sentenced, 'not so much for what he might have done, as for being a symbol of something which the contemporary public found abhorrent and threatening to their stable way of life'.[20] This line of thought was quite apparent in much of the sentencing in the nineteenth century and will be studied further in Chapter 8.

On the basis that the model of folk devils and moral panics has current relevance, the question that remains is how powerful was the press in the nineteenth century? The power of the press depends on its influence – both on public opinion and on the government. In a democracy its influence depends on how far the press can claim to represent public opinion and to what extent it can mould it. Only if the press was capable of significantly influencing Victorian society could it act in the role of effective moral entrepreneur. There is evidence that newspapers were highly influential during the nineteenth century and were not averse to using their influence to alter certain aspects of society. It is to the questions of the source of this influence and its use that the following sections are addressed.

IV

It is the function of supplying information and a forum for the airing of views that led many nineteenth-century writers to refer to the press as the Fourth Estate. In 1871 James Grant wrote that, 'within the last few years the appellation of 'The Fourth Estate' given to our newspaper journalism, has acquired an appropriateness to which it was never entitled at any previous period of its history'.[21] It was widely believed that, 'if by accident journalism were to become suddenly extinct, such a Parliamentary Reform as the wildest of us have never dreamed of, would be an instant and paramount necessity'.[22] In 1860 the lack of a popular outcry over the Reform Question after the withdrawal of Russell's Reform Bill was explained by the existence of a free press through whose agency, 'the influence of Public Opinion is brought to bear on the Government and the Legislature, and thus renders the existence of a House of Commons on the basis of extended suffrage less necessary'.[23] Henry Reeve, writing in 1855, believed that 'newspapers are just as truly representative of the people as legal senators' so that their 'influence is scarcely possible to exaggerate. Journalism is now truly an estate of the realm; more powerful than any of the other estates'.[24] There is much evidence to support the latter contention that the press was the most powerful of the estates.

The first leading article of the *Saturday Review* by editor John Douglas Cook stated, 'No apology is necessary for assuming that this country is ruled by *The Times*'.[25] From 1820 onwards *The Times* seemed to many to speak with the voice of public opinion and the editors of the new cheap press were referred to as 'the new school of would-be directors of opinion'.[26] The crucial point was that London newspapers were recognised as the vehicle of national public opinion despite Reid's observation that '*The Times* and its ring of contemporaries do not accurately express the opinion of the public' but merely 'convey to us with admirable force and accuracy the opinions of Pall Mall, or of the Lobby, or of the cultural circles in which they themselves move'.[27] The power of *The Times* was criticised by Henry Reeve in 1855. He believed that a paper with the monopoly of *The Times* 'of itself forms, and is, the public opinion of the country.'[28]

It has been argued in the previous chapter that criminal statistics and their publication were events in themselves. The *Saturday Review* credited *The Times* with the same distinction in 1858:

> In undertaking the task of reviewing the events of the week, we cannot omit to criticise writings which are themselves events, and which, as each breakfast hour returns, exercise so enormous an influence on English opinion and English character ... the events which never fail are the leading articles of *The Times*.'[29]

It was not only the leading articles of *The Times* that were influential. E.P. Thompson believes that in times of perceived adversity the middle classes will actually articulate their values and commitments and that, 'one infallible signal of such a time of bourgeois renaissance is the epistolary levée en masse of the readers of *The Times*'. Thompson notes the infrequency of such outbursts and cites the outcry following the Trafalgar Square riot of February 1886 as a fine example.[30]

The press had therefore developed as a powerful institution with a reputation for representing public opinion and carrying out the function of the Fourth Estate. This placed the press in a position whereby it could play a large part in the formulation of the public opinion which it claimed to reflect. In 1886 W.T. Stead described the ability of an editor to generate public opinion – 'the greatest force of politics' – and claimed he had seen 'cabinets upset, ministers driven into retirement, laws repealed, great social reforms initiated, Bills transformed, estimates re-modelled, programmes modified, Acts passed, generals nominated, governors appointed, armies sent hither and thither, war proclaimed and war averted, by the agency of newspapers'.[31] Stead also described the method by which a minister wishing to push through a social reform would persuade acquaintances to button-hole a few journalists and persuade them to support the reform in their columns. The minister could then declare that 'public support had spoken in its favour' whilst knowing that the so-called public opinion was nothing more than the printed reproduction of his own words.

Many editors saw the influence of the press as a gradual process, almost a war of attrition against the readership. Barnes, influential editor of *The Times*, observed that 'John Bull, whose understanding is rather sluggish ... requires a strong stimulus ... you must fire ten-pounders at his densely compacted intellect before you make him comprehend your meaning'.[32] J.A Roebuck, writing in 1832, also held the view that newspaper influence had to be built-up over years with constant repetition of arguments. 'It is the dropping of water on stone, the line upon line, the precept upon precept, that brings about important changes. The people can be effectually moved only by being constantly addrssed'.[33] Such daily poundings of the readership built up a fund of influence on which newspapers could occasionally draw to bring about change. This was the case with the London garotting panics of 1856 and 1862.

V

In July 1851, four letters were published in *The Times*, all from victims of garotte attacks, two of which implied that such crimes were being concealed by the police and were on the increase. In retrospect this appeared to be a subconscious testing of the temperature of public opinion on the subject which did not bring much reaction. The subject was not yet worthy of public debate by the respectable section of society although the police were constantly, 'pelted by the lower organs of the press, which finds no subject so agreeable to their readers in the dull season as 'pitching into the police' ...'.[34]

It was in the winter of 1856 and the spring of 1857 that *The Times* mounted its first major attack on the garotter and the system of justice which allowed him free reign in the capital. Between 31 October and 31 December 1856 there were seven editorials each approximately 1,200 words in length on the subject of crime. The first[35] observed the increase of garotting and called for the renewal of capital punishment. The second followed a speech by Palmerston in Manchester in which he declared that Britons were safe to travel throughout the world. *The Times* replied that, 'it is of far more moment to a Londoner that he should at all hours of the day or night walk safely in the streets of London' and referred to areas 'inhabited by a numerous and respectable' population where a man cannot walk, 'without imminent danger of being throttled, robbed, and, if not actually murdered, at least kicked and pommelled within an inch of his life'. *The Times* foresaw the panic which it was to be partly responsible for creating and warned that, 'apprehension will rise to a higher pitch than even the outrages actually perpetrated will justify'.[36] The paper called for more gas-lamps, more police and a tightening of the ticket-of-leave system as 'these thieves and garotters must be put down'. The remaining five editorials called for a new system of transportation for 'that portion of our community that subsists by strangling and robbing the remainder'[37] and warning that the present system of punishment would break down given more garotte robberies and burglaries. Letters from philanthropists and liberal penal reformers such as Matthew Davenport-Hill, R. Monckton Milnes and George S. Jenkinson brought forth immediate condemnatory editorials often with the message that the 'annual discharge of burglars and garotters' preyed on the innocent who could not afford it and that rich philosophers who wished to experiment should take garotters home and pay for their support without burdening the state.[38]

Between 31 October 1856 and 23 February 1857 *The Times* published thirty-one letters on the subject, several of which acknowledged the power of the paper for 'by the public voice it appears that *The Times* is the great redresser of evils'[39] and 'it is well-known that your mighty organ is the only way of giving their rights to the London public'.[40] Of these letters five were from liberal reformers, four attacked the police for inactivity, five described garotte attacks and one, forwarded by the police, admitted that the writer's report of a garotte was falsely made for, having dined with a friend, he had 'taken too much wine'. Seven correspondents believed that the attacks should be countered with a variety of methods of self-protection. Eight correspondents urged transportation for criminals and commented on the failure of the ticket-of-leave system, and several called for the reinstatement of hanging. Others made observations on the efffect of education and model prisons on criminals and suggestions for employing criminals after their discharge. Most of the letters were written in measured tone – that from 'A Ticket-of-Leave Holder' so measured as to be scarcely credible – although it was 'The London Scoundrel' who probably truly reflected the editorial views of the paper:-

Away with maudlin sympathy and twaddle. When a ruffian watches for you at night, fractures your skull, lacerates your windpipe, or clogs your brain with apoplectic blood, hang him, if you are lucky enough to catch him. Shoot him at the time if you can, but, if not, hang him.[41]

By late December 1856 R. Monckton Milnes admitted that 'public opinion is just now running strong in favour of additional severity of punishment'[42] and 'S.G.O.' looking forward to the next session of parliament hoped for 'some measures which may allow of our going . . . for a walk in London, without justifiable fear of being found the next day a spectacle for the coroner'.[43] The legislation, even if not entirely satisfactory, was to come in the form of the Penal Servitude Act of 1857.

In November and December 1862, *The Times* renewed its attack. Another outbreak of reports of garotting led it once again to direct its attention to the system of secondary punishments. Eighteen editorials argued for the return of transportation. The number of police reports increased and Robert Montagu, MP, observed that 'those persons who do not read those reports have had their attention directed to those appalling facts by leading articles in your paper'.[44] On 5 November 1862 the campaign opened with the warning that, 'now the long nights are coming we shall have to buy revolvers and carry them in our pockets'. The editor harangued the law, the police, magistrates and judges and especially the Home Secretary and the gaol chaplains. 'The whole of this great and most expensive judicial hierarchy seems to be established solely to catch thieves and let them go again'. Two days later the paper stated that, 'men are garotted and robbed in the most public and well-frequented thoroughfares' and 'we believe that impunity has been at the bottom of the mischief'. In this period there were only ten letters on the subject, three reporting garotte incidents, one recommending the use of the bludgeon for self-protection, one recommending the punishment of flogging and the rest urging the resumption of transportation and discussing the relative merits of Labrador, the Falkland Islands, Queensland and the Cameroon Mountains for the establishment of a penal colony. *The Times* relied almost entirely on the use of its leading articles to forward its case and attack any dissenters. Mr Russell Gurney, the recorder at the Central Criminal Court, told the Court that the vast increase in street robbery cases before the Court could be partly accounted for by an increase in police efficiency. *The Times* remonstrated that, 'if street robberies had been at all common ten years ago, we should infallibly have heard of them' and went on categorically to state that, 'we hear of them now, not because the offenders are caught but because the offence is an everyday matter'.[45] Sir Joshua Jebb, the

Director of Prisons, write a letter defending the ticket-of-leave system and disputing the assertion that garotting was a result of the system. *The Times* referred to the convicts as 'these pampered ruffians' who are the 'bravoes and throttlers who infest our streets'. This was a fact acknowledged by 'every Recorder, every criminal lawyer, every gaoler, every detective policemen'. The increase in police reports shows 'the notorious truth. Yet in the middle of all this a placid theorist comes boldly forward, and calmly assures us that the universal belief is the universal delusion'.[46] The paper had already warned that 'while prison theorists are wrangling honest people get their throats cut'.[47] Several judges had commented that the system of secondary punishment was not severe enough and it was 'the present insecurity of life and property in the very streets of the metropolis' which occasioned such comment.[48]

On 28 November 1862 Robert Montagu, MP, argued that the police force was too small and too ill-paid to carry out proper surveillance of convicts released on licence and called for a parliamentary committee of inquiry into the condition and requirements of the Metropolitan Police. On 6 December 'A Chairman of Quarter Sessions' noted that flogging must be introduced for robbery with violence – a cry to be taken up in the editorial columns of *The Times* of spring 1863 (see Chapter 7). By 10 December the editor believed that, 'there seems already to be a pretty general agreement on the nature of the reform required in our Penal System' and that 'Penal Servitude, in short, as now administered, is confessed to be a mockery'. It is an interesting comment on the power of the press that although the police escaped unscathed Sir George Grey, the Home Secretary, announced in December 1862 the setting up of a Royal Commission on Penal Servitude and Transportation which reported in June 1863 and led to the Penal Servitude Act of 1864. There was also a Select Committee of the House of Lords on the Present State of Discipline in Gaols and Houses of Correction which reported in July 1863, resulting in the Prisons Act of 1865 and in July 1863 the Security from Violence Act was passed to bring back flogging for crimes of robbery with violence.

VI

By the 1850s and 1860s several factors had come together to create mass media which were not only more efficient as media but also more capable of reaching the masses. The press had developed a format which would not be further modernised until Harmsworth broke through into the true mass circulation that we know today. Technological advances and alterations in the system of indirect taxation allowed the production of many more copies of newspapers than had been possible in the first half of the century at a drastically reduced cost. Under the influence of *The Times* the press was accepted as an institution that was influential in augmenting change in society. The new journalism, with its commercial approach, reached a mass market the very size of which represented its influence. The newspaper press was ready to carry out its first real act of moral enterprise. All that was needed was an initial deviance, at the right time and correctly handled, for the Victorians to experience their first moral panic. This initial deviance and potential initial deviances are the subject of Chapter 4.

Notes

1. S. Cohen, *Folk Devils and Moral Panics: The Creation of the Mods and Rockers* (1972), and S. Cohen and J. Young (eds), *The Manufacture of News: Deviance, Social Problems and the Mass Media* (1973).
2. Cohen, op.cit., (1972) 9.
3. See E. Larsen, *Telecommunications: A History*, (1977).
4. See R. Williams, *The Long Revolution*, (1961).
5. See V. Berridge, 'Popular Sunday Papers and Mid-Victorian Society', in G. Boyce, J. Curran and P. Wingate (eds), *Newspaper History from the Seventeenth-Century to the Present Day*, (1978).
6. P.J. Lucas, 'Furness Newspapers in Mid-Victorian England', in S.P. Bell (ed.), *Victorian Lancashire* (1974)
7. Williams, op.cit., 195.
8. J.W. Robertson Scott, *The Life and Death of a Newspaper* (1952), 157.
9. E.F.L. Burnham, *Peterborough Court: The Story of the Daily Telegraph* (1955)
10. Berridge, op.cit.
11. R. Roshier, 'The Selection of Crime News by the Press' in Cohen and Young, op.cit. and F.J. Davis, 'Crime News in Colorado Newspapers', *American Journal of Sociology*, LVII (June 1952) 325–330.
12. W.T. Stead, 'Government by Journalism', *Contemporary Review*, 49 January to June (1886).
13. 'Moral Enterprise' was a term coined by Howard S. Becker in *Outsiders: Studies in the Sociology of Deviance* (1963), to refer to individuals who, once a problem has been spotlighted, seize on the problem, amplify it and conduct a public campaign calling on the legal authorities to take a more active stance in relation to the problem. Such entrepreneurs may be viewed as right-thinking 'muck-rakers'.
14. Report of the Select Committee on Newspaper Stamps, *Parliamentary Papers* (1851) XXVII, questions 600 and 604.
15. A. Smith, 'The Long Road to Objectivity and Back Again: The Kinds of Truth we get in Journalism', in Boyce, et al., op.cit.

16. *Annual Review*, 1862.
17. W. Bent, *Criminal Life: Reminiscences of Forty-Two Years as a Police Officer*, (1891), 220.
18. *The Times*, 17 December 1874.
19. P.R.O., *Central Criminal Court Calendars*
20. A. Parker, *The Plough Boy* (1965), 235.
21. J. Grant, *The Newspaper Press* (1871) Vol. II, 459.
22. H. Reeve, 'The Newspaper Press', *Edinburgh Review*, 102, October 1855, 479.
23. *Leicester Chronicle*, 16 June 1860
24. Reeve, op.cit., 481 and 477.
25. *Saturday Review*, 3 November 1855.
26. *The Times, The History of the Times; 1841–84* (1939) Vol. II, 300.
27. T. Wemyss Reid, 'Public Opinion and Its Leaders', *Fortnightly Review* 28, (1880), 234 and 243.
28. Reeve, op.cit., 492.
29. *Saturday Review*, 16 January, 1858.
30. E.P. Thompson, 'Sir, Writing by Candlelight', *New Society*, 24 December 1970, 1135–36.
31. W.T. Stead, 'Government by Journalism', *Contemporary Review*, 49, January – June 1886, 661 and 664.
32. R. Waters, 'Thomas Barnes and "The Times", 1817–41', *History Today*, 29 September 1979, 561–8.
33. D. Read, *Press and People, 1790 – 1850* (1961), 207.
34. 'The Police of London', *Quarterly Review*, 129, 1870.
35. *The Times*, 5 November 1856.
36. *The Times*, 5 December, 1856.
37. *The Times*, 18 November, 1856.
38. See for example, *The Times*, 18 November, 5 December, 17 December, 24 December, 1856.
39. Letter from 'Anti-Garotter', *The Times*, 11 November, 1856.
40. Letter from 'One who has a great objection to being garotted', *The Times*, 31 October 1856.
41. Letter from 'The London Scoundrel', *The Times*, 16 December 1856.
42. Letter from R. Monckton Milnes, *The Times* 24 December 1856.
43. Letter from 'S.G.O.', *The Times*, 26 December 1856.
44. Letter from Robert Montagu, MP, *The Times*, 28 November 1862.
45. *The Times*, 26 November 1862.
46. *The Times*, 21 November 1862.
47. *The Times*, 11 November.
48. *The Times*, 5 December 1862.

4. The Initial Deviance – The Scares

I

The creation of a moral panic requires an initial deviance which may be viewed as an excuse for the focusing of attention by the press on phenomena which may have been long in existence. In the case of a phenomenon such as street violence, which had existed for some time, Cohen's flow model of an initial deviance leading to an inventory and sensitisation may be reversed so that the inventory may be built up over a period of time by reference to events of which the readership is aware but does not regard as any cause for alarm. This preparation of the ground then gives the initial deviance greater impact when the press choose to present it as if it were the volcano which has always been there and has only just now erupted in the middle of society. By educating its readership as to the significance of key words such as outrage, rough and garotte, the press build up an inventory and create a sensitisation which gives the reporting of the initial deviance a far greater impact. This process of inventory creation is discernible in the press from 1851 to 1856, prior to the panics of 1856 and 1862 which stemmed from an over-estimation of the deviance and resulted in changes in the control culture. The provincial outbreaks of the reporting of street violence never had the same impact as their metropolitan counterparts. The provincial press spent less time preparing the ground and were never likely to bring about changes in the legislature. Their attempts at panic creation were more limited both in effort and objective. The embarrassment of the chairmen of watch committees or the improvement of conditions in one small area of a town would be regarded as a victory for the provincial press. It was the metropolitan press which reported national outbreaks and called for changes in national laws and policies and so it was the metropolitan press which created the true moral panics which helped in a small way to alter society in nineteenth-century Britain.

Alexander Andrews proclaimed in 1859 that 'the list of our public journals is a proud and noble list ... It is a police of public safety and a sentinel of public morals'.[1] In the same year the *Morning Post* also evinced the belief that the press had a role to play as moral censor and the ability to focus attention on what the press arbitrarily perceived as deviations from public morals. It believed that in civilised cities such as London and Paris, 'Owing to the revelations of the press and the police, there is an immense flood of light thrown on all deviations from the moral law'.[2] The *Morning Post* believed that if the press were to give publicity to remote districts the proportionate amount of crime would be as great as in the cities, thereby arguing that the level of crime in the public mind was in fact the level of reporting of crime by the press. This line of argument is supported by Wilfred Hindle's reference to a member of parliament giving 'a reassurance to those whom the newspapers had caused to fear the progress of crime'.[3] This is a basic premise of this study – that if the press does not report an event then in the public mind the event did not take place, but if the press reports the event and exaggerates it then the event is exaggerated in the public mind. It is to a number of these exaggeratedly-reported events to which our attention is now turned. Their effect on the public mind will be studied in the following chapters.

II

The first foray into moral entrepreneurship with regard to street violence came with a small series of letters in *The Times* in 1851. The criminal statistics provide no evidence as to the timing of this outburst. The number of people charged with street violence offences in London had increased slightly from 88 (4.8 per cent of the total commitments) in 1850 to 91 (5.4 per cent of the total commitments) in 1851. This does not seem to be a newsworthy increase.

On 2 January 1851 an article entitled 'New System of Robbery' appeared in *The Times* describing a classic garotte attack on a gentleman at Victoria railway station, Manchester. By December 1851, *The Times* noted under the heading, 'The Garotte in Birmingham' that the 'garotte robberies unhappily continue on the increase' and that the 'frequency of these attacks, and the audacious manner in which they are carried on, cause great alarm to the inhabitants of the town'.[4] It was in July that a series of letters was printed although there were only eight committals for street violence in London that month compared to nine in April, fifteen in June, sixteen in August and eleven in October. 'A Sufferer' who was garotted and robbed of his watch and chain and of £4 explained that this 'atrocious attack' had taken place in a public thoroughfare and observed that 'these diabolical robberies are not of rare occurrence';[5] and 'A victim of Thuggee' wrote of the 'increasing frequency and boldness of the new system of robbery'.[6]

In 1851, and later in 1856, the initial deviance was something which had been in existence long enough, but suddenly appeared in the limelight. It was the beginning of the process of firing ten-pounders at the densely compacted intellect of John Bull in order to create the inventory. The 1851 contributions to the inventory were that these attacks could occur in public thoroughfares and the victims were often of the social class from which the readership of *The Times* was drawn. These two facts were enough to reclassify a mere crime as an 'outrage'. Robberies are now diabolical, attacks are atrocious and, of course, all outrages are serious.

From 1851 to 1856 the process of 'dropping water on stone, the line upon line' proceeded. There was no moral panic but a steady reporting of the phenomenon of garotting. The inventory was built slowly leading to the moral panic of 1856 and then the process repeated itself prior to the moral panic of 1862. W.L. Clay, writing in 1862, observed the process happening. 'If things continue in their present course', he wrote, 'we may look for another panic ere long. The subsidence of that in 1856 was as irrational as its rise'.[7]

On 27 May Mr. F.W. Mablethorpe, a young clerk in Hull, achieved the dubious distinction of being the first fatality as a result of garotting. Robbed of a gold watch and £11, 'the external appearance of the body indicated that death had been occasioned by suffocation, no marks of violence being observed, but some scratches as of human nails upon each cheek'.[8] Also in 1852 Leeds received its full measure of reports of garottes. *The Times*, 12 July 1852 reported that, 'many and daring have been the robberies of this character perpetrated in this neighbourhood during the last winter'. The robberies continued and *The Times* noted that, 'Leeds is gaining an unenviable notoriety for the frequency and reckless character of garotte robberies in its vicinities'.[9] Police said that the West Riding and Borough of Leeds Quarter Sessions had just concluded 'and some few ''well-known characters'', as the police say, have been set at liberty in the course of the sessional proceedings'.[10] Such a comment intimates that a pyramidal concept of blame was present. The public blamed the police who in turn blamed the courts. It also illustrates an addition to the inventory which was to be a central theme of the moral panic of 1856. It was believed that there was a finite number of ruffians, a specific section of the 'dangerous class' whose trade was garotter and that the incarceration of this section would solve the problem. It was part of the folklore that as fast as the police were capturing garotters the judicial system was releasing others who had served their sentence. In the minds of many of the public the idea grew that this problem could only be solved by much longer terms of penal servitude or the reintroduction of capital punishment for such offences. Another aspect of the inventory which was built up during the 1850s was that garotting was spreading. No longer confined to the rough quarters of large cities, where the middle classes were unaffected, the garotte was sweeping the country. Throughout the 1850s all the major cities and many lesser towns were reported as experiencing isolated outbreaks of garotting. However, the outbreaks of reports from the provinces tended to be sporadic and isolated. The main wave of reports focused on the metropolis and these reached their height in 1856.

It was in 1856 that the first moral panic with the press acting as moral entrepreneurs occurred. Its effect on the legislative arm of the control culture is fully described in Chapter 8. Throughout 1856 the number of reports of garottings appearing in the press increased and the cause was pleaded to be the number of convicts released on parole with a ticket-of-leave. On 27 September 1856 a mock advertisement for an Anti-Garotte Collar appeared in *Punch*.

Tables 4.1 and 4.2 show that there was some statistical justification for a heightened interest in the amount of violence in the winter of 1856. The 1857 figures, which run from September 1856, show that although there was a substantial decrease in the total number of committals (a fall of 24.4 per cent since 1850 and 15.5 per cent since 1855) there was a marked increase in the total number of offences against the person (increased by 13.1 per cent since 1855 and 14.4 per cent since 1850). The most notable of the figures were the 31.4 per cent increase since 1855 in the number of assaults with intent to rob and demanding money with menaces and the 40.4 per cent increase of robbery, and attempts to rob, by persons armed and in company. Against a trend of falling committals there was an increase in the two main categories of offences against the person and offences against property with violence. How much of this increase was a result of sensitisation is impossible to say, although the 100.5 per cent increase in the number of common assaults from 1855 to 1857 offers a clue. It is unlikely that the number of assaults actually doubled. Summary courts, conscious of the growing public outcry, were probably sending more cases to the Quarter Sessions and Assizes so that heavier sentences could be given with the result that the number of committals for trial was increased and the panic further fuelled. As has been argued in an earlier chapter, the factual basis of the statistics is not necessarily important. The statistics themselves form the factual basis for a panic.

The judiciary began to react to the panic and it was Mr Baron

Table 4.1 Extracts from comparative tables of the number of persons committed or bailed for trial 1850 to 1865 and the offences with which the persons stood charged

	1850	1851	1852	1853	1854	1855	1856	1857	1858	1859	1860	1861	1862	1863	1864	1865
Total offences against the person	1,866	2,218	2,241	2,400	1,849	1,908	1,919	2,158	2,145	2,019	1,802	2,058	2,212	2,655	2,644	2,577
Assault and inflicting bodily harm	607	91	321	362	276	303	332	345	414	365	342	422	596	775	775	664
Assaults (common)		661	434	378	339	198	258	397	280	292	208	305	236	260	283	262
Total offences against property with violence	2,014	2,060	1,975	1,696	1,770	1,728	2,258	2,290	1,897	1,546	1,424	1,970	2,321	2,198	2,053	1,979
Burglary attended with violence to persons	5	18	16	6	6	2	25	8	19	7	NO LONGER LISTED SEPARATELY					
Robbery and attempts to rob, by persons armed, in company, etc.	319	350	406	372	293	322	317	452	335	267	247	287	318	360	411	370
Robbery, attended with cutting and wounding	12	16	13	16	9	14	3	13	7	3	NO LONGER LISTED SEPARATELY					
Assaults, to rob, and demanding money with menaces	38	37	38	38	28	35	40	46	34	42	42	41	70	48	31	44
Grand total of all committals	26,813	27,960	27,510	27,057	29,359	25,072	19,437	20,269	17,855	16,674	15,999	18,326	20,001	20,819	19,506	18,614

Source: Judicial Statistics 1859 P.P. 1860 LXLV 473, 54, and Judicial Statistics 1866 P.P. 1867 LXVI 523, 52.

Table 4.2 Percentage movements comparing 1857 to 1850 and 1855

	Per cent 1857 cf. 1850	Per cent 1857 cf. 1855
Total offences against the person	14.4	13.1
Assault, and inflicting bodily harm		13.8
Assaults (common)	22.2	100.5
Total offences against property with violence	13.7	32.5
Burglary, attended with violence to persons	60.0	400.0
Robbery and attempts to rob, by persons armed, etc.	41.7	40.4
Robbery attended with wounding or cutting	8.0	–7.0
Assaults, to rob, and demanding property with menaces	21.0	31.4
Grand total of all committals	–24.4	–15.5

Source: Table 4.1

Watson on 26 November 1856, who donned the mantle of folk hero by giving the press and the public the satisfaction of a heavy sentence. Charles Hunter and Thomas Murty were sentenced to transportation for life following a garotte attack. *The Times* reported, 'the sentence evidently filled them with a terror' and gleefully proclaimed that, 'garotters may expect, in future, no mercy from either the courts of justice or the public'.[11]

The *Globe* newspaper, surveying the cases of garotting examined by the Southwark and Greenwich magistrates, came to three conclusions about the garotters. The first added to the symbolisation by stating it as a fact that the thieves displayed a 'cowardly character' as is 'sufficiently manifest from the fact that there are always two, often three, engaged in these villainous proceedings'. Secondly, it was concluded that in most cases the attack could have been prevented if the victim had himself carried an offensive weapon. This theme of self-protection will be studied in the next chapter, but is evidence of the fact that public opinion had not then reached the twentieth-century attitude of total reliance on the establishment forces of law enforcement and protection. Thirdly, the inventory was reinforced by comment on the arbitrary nature of the attacks, and the fact that 'the street Bedouins lurk in the highways and rob great and small alike ... Risk their liberties – it may be their necks – on the chance of getting something'.[12]

Added to this arbitrariness was the fact that attacks were being reported from largely middle-class residential districts, thus adding to the perennial and accepted violence of the traditional areas of the lower socio-economic groups. This was the geographical facet of people who did not know their place in society. 'Success and impunity have apparently made these rascals so bold', wailed a contributor to *The Times* letter columns, 'that they no longer confine their operations to by-lanes but attack us in the most frequented thoroughfares of the metropolis'.[13] This was not only worrying to the readership of *The Times*, it constituted an attack on (middle-class) society's values. Each person should know their place, both geographically and socially, and if this was ceasing to be the case then society was beginning to break down.

The 1856 panic subsided and the number of reports in the newspapers diminished. Some half-hearted attempts at legislative change gave the newspapers a reason to drop the campaign which could not maintain its newsworthiness during the spring months. In 1862 the reports began again and a full blown moral panic ensued.

III

The London garotte panic of 1862–63 differed from that of 1856 in two main respects. First there seemed to be an awareness of the panic itself and secondly it was provoked by a definite initial deviance which made it far more intense than its predecessor and temporally easier to define.

W.L. Clay had forecast the panic in 1861 and Matthew Davenport-Hill had waited for it as the stimulus to change penal legislation. He viewed the 'terrible outbreak of garotting which created a panic from Land's End to John O'Groats' as the cogent influence needed to move the legislature.[14] All seemed in agreement that the social adrenalin was flowing and focusing the public mind on the criminal question. 'Garotting is the talk of the town, penal jurisprudence the favourite after-dinner topic',[15] observed the *Illustrated London News*. The *Shoreditch Advertiser* noted 'the public mind has been thrown into a state of great alarm by the numerous reports of the cases of violent robbery which have been set afloat during the last few months'.[16] The *Weekly Dispatch* reported that the criminal question had been 'pressed upon the public attention by the alarming increase of thefts, robberies, violent assaults and murders',[17] whilst a contributor to *Reynolds' Newspaper* believed that the garotter had proved that the combined efforts of the established Church, the police and the army were 'not equal to the task of protecting society'.[18]

The panic started at one o'clock on the morning of 17 July 1862, and ended gradually with the imprisonment of twenty-seven garotters at the November sessions of the Central Criminal Court, the giving of the Royal Assent to the Security from Violence Act on 13 July 1863 and the announcement of a Royal Commission to inquire into transportation and penal servitude on 23 December 1862.

The panic started with a late sitting of the House of Commons. Mr Pilkington, the member for Blackburn, was attacked by two men on his way home at one in the morning. He was robbed of £10 and a watch. Five policemen were close to the scene of the attack but heard nothing.

The following day, in the House, Lord Lennox asked Sir George Grey, the Home Secretary, if he was aware of the attack. Grey replied that immediately on hearing of the attack he had sent to the police authorities for their report on the matter. The report gave a similar account to that which had appeared in the press.[19] About a month later two men were charged with the assault on Pilkington, at Marlborough Police Court on the evidence of a prostitute. The evidence, however, was contradictory and unsupported and the men were discharged. The Pilkington case gained immortality by forming the basis for the attack on the cabinet minister, Mr Kennedy, described in Anthony Trollope's *Phineas Finn* first published serially in *St Paul's Magazine* from October 1867.

In addition to this well-publicised initial deviance. Tables 4.1 and 4.3 show that there was, superficially, some statistical justification for the panic which did not really commence until the final quarter of 1862.

Against the background of a falling crime rate the number of offences against the person had risen by 40.8 per cent since 1850, and by 11 per cent over the previous year. Committals for assault had increased by 70.5 per cent since 1850 and by a remarkable 31.7 per cent since the previous year for assault and inflicting bodily harm. Robbery and attempts to rob showed an increase of 11.5 per cent in one year. As can be seen from Table 4.4, the committals for trial had fallen when compared to 1850 although they had reached a low in 1860 and were beginning to rise gradually by 1863. However, compared to the late 1840s and early 1850s the figures for total committals did not give a

Table 4.3 Percentage movements comparing 1863 to 1850 and 1862

	Per cent 1863 cf. 1850	Per cent 1863 cf. 1862
Total offences against the person	40.8	11.0
Assault, and inflicting bodily harm		31.7
Assaults (common)	70.5	10.2
Total offences against property with violence	−29.3	−5.3
Robbery and attempts to rob, by persons armed, etc.	12.9	11.7
Assaults, to rob, and demanding property with menaces	26.3	−31.4
Grand total of all committals	−22.4	4.1

Source: Table 4.1

Table 4.4 Number sent for trial in England and Wales

Year	No. for Trial	Year	No. for Trial
1844	26,342	1854	29,359
1845	24,303	1855	25,072
1846	23,107	1856	19,437
1847	28,833	1857	20,267
1848	30,349	1858	17,855
1849	27,816	1859	16,674
1850	26,813	1860	15,999
1851	27,960	1861	18,326
1852	27,510	1862	20,001
1853	27,057	1863	20,819

Source: Judicial Statistics 1863, Parliamentary Papers 1864, LVII, 445 p. xx.

Table 4.5 Number of crimes committed and the number of persons apprehended in England and Wales 1862/1863

	Crimes Committed	Persons Apprehended
October, November, December	14,356	8,195
January, February, March	13,606	7,719
April, May, June	12,380	7,407
July, August, September	11,869	7,689
	52,211	30,010

Source: Judicial Statistics 1863, Parliamentary Papers 1864, LVII, 445, p. xi.

picture of a criminal population which was posing an especial threat to society.

Table 4.5 reveals that it was the winter of 1862 when the largest number of crimes was committed. The greatest number of crimes are always committed in the winter quarters mainly owing to the longer hours of darkness and possibly the greater amount of seasonal unemployment combined with the hostile weather increasing the deprivations of the poor. However, the Home Office observed that the numbers in the last three months of 1862 was higher than the winter quarters for the preceding few years. This was followed by a considerable decrease in the first quarter of 1863 and for July, August and September of 1863 the figures were lower than for the corresponding months of any of the three preceding years.[21]

The figures for those sent to trial are open to the interpretation that they were influenced by the reporting of the initial deviance and the subsequent escalation of police activity. Those for the number of crimes committed cannot be dismissed so easily because the rule that statistics closer to the actual event tend to be more accurate holds good. However, it may be argued that during this period people felt more encouraged to report crimes so that the level of reporting was increased and the dark number thereby reduced. This lowering of the dark number may have had a significant effect on the figures but the fact remains that the figures were high. In the winter of 1862 and the first three quarters of 1863 there were 755 serious cases of assault (cf. 504 in 1862) in England and Wales, 783 robberies and attempts to rob on the highway (cf. 566 in 1862) and the total number of assaults dealt with summarily increased by 7,349 or

9.2 per cent over 1862, which itself had been an increase of 2,695 or 3.4 per cent over 1861.[22]

The geographical source of these 1862 statistics highlights the importance of London in the press. For robbery on the highway and attempts to rob there were 242 cases in the Counties, 351 in the Boroughs, 143 in the Metropolitan Police District and 2 in the City of London. Of these, 262 offences occurred in Lancashire, 34 being reported by the County Constabulary and 228 by the Borough Police. In Liverpool there were 17 cases and 167 in Manchester. The majority of serious assaults occurred in Liverpool (167) followed by the Metropolitan Police District (143) and Manchester (53). The distribution is interesting as the panic had a distinct Metropolitan bias although the statistics point to the North-West as the main centre of street violence. There was none of the humorous comment in the press about Liverpudlians which characterised the specifically Liverpudlian phenomenon of cornermen in the 1870s. This may be accounted for by the majority of middle-class victims being in the Metropolis for it was there that the criminal elements showed signs of spilling out of their traditional areas. Any further analysis would be erroneous because of the in-built defects of the criminal statistics. There was, for example, probably a major discrepancy in definition as to what constituted robbery on the highway or serious assault between the constabularies and justices of London, Liverpool and Manchester.

However valid the statistical justification of the panic, the panic itself was real enough. Representative of the writing of this period was the statement by the *Daily News* that London was 'a battlefield of raging cabmen by day and a lair of footpads and assassins by night'[23] while the *Quarterly Review* was of the opinion that the 'streets of the Metropolis are not safe even in the day time'.[24] At the height of the panic *The Times* spoke of 'the present insecurity of life and property in the very streets of the Metropolis'[25] whilst *All Year Round* observed that people were thinking twice before choosing their route home and were becoming very wary of being followed for the news of all the garottes 'has created quite a panic in the town'.[26] Much of the panic literature revealed an existing situation rather than a phenomenon.

The panic both produced and was fed by rumours and plain fictions masqueraded as fact. This was the process of the inventory and sensitisation which fed back on each other to produce an overestimation of the deviance. Every attack was published as a garotte and on an individual level it was not unknown for two perfectly innocent citizens to attack each other, both thinking that they were pre-empting a garotte. In December 1962 the police issued a statement that they believed the attacker of a certain Mr Holland was not a garotter but 'probably thinking that he himself was going to be attacked'.[27] This was a favourite theme of *Punch* cartoons – men running from their shadows, imagining trees to be garotters in the fog, etc. The *Shoreditch Advertiser* put the factual basis of the reports in truer perspective. The paper believed that garotting had increased but that at least 10 per cent of the reports were false. Having investigated all the instances reported in Shoreditch they could not trace one to a legitimate source, all turning out to be 'utterly fictitious or mere drunken squabbles'.[28]

The November sessions of the Central Criminal Court in 1862 marked the high point of the establishment's offensive against the garotters. In June 1863 Sir Richard Mayne, Commissioner of the Metropolitan Police, told Lord Carnavon that the 27 garotters who appeared before Baron Bramwell probably accounted for nearly all the 82 robberies with violence which had occurred in the Metropolis in the last six months of 1862.[29] The *Annual Review* for 1862 took the same view and felt that the police had either captured all the garotters or that the sentences had terrorised their colleagues as they believed the violence stopped as of that date. Not everyone took that simplistic view. For example, a Chairman of Quarter Sessions argued that attacks were rife on the night that Bramwell passed sentence thus proving penal servitude was ineffective and he called for the return of flogging.[30]

Following the November sessions of the Central Criminal Court and the parting comments of the press throughout December, the press coverage of street violence markedly declined. Press attention turned to the revolution in Greece, the capture of Garibaldi in Italy, the distress in Lancashire and the progress of the American War.

In June 1863 *The Times*, in a leader to celebrate the reading of the Security from Violence Bill, looked back on the garotte outbreak and felt that it had declined as a result of more daylight, increased vigilance of the police, the exceptional severity in the application of the existing law and a 'strongly manifested determination on the part of the public'.[31] These are quite convincing and plausible reasons for the cessation of robbery with violence, although it was the reports that ceased and not the actual crimes. The more newsworthy events in Italy, Greece, America and Lancashire were more probably the real reason for the decline in interest in robbery with violence.

IV

William Bent recalled in his reminiscences of his life as a police officer an outbreak of robbery with violence, 'about the year 1865, not only in Manchester and Salford, but throughout the neighbourhood and all over Lancashire'. Bent stated that the number of attacks grew so rapidly that it became 'unsafe for any person to walk alone through any but the best lighted and most frequented thoroughfares'.[32] Bent's information is, in parts, inaccurate. He recalled that the outbreak was stopped by 'the courageous hand of a strong administrator' who, 'seeing the necessity of crushing the outrage, brought to bear the "cat"'. This, he believed, was the work of Mr Justice Lush at the Manchester Assizes in August 1865. In fact Justice Lush came to Manchester for the first time to preside over the Salford Hundred of Lancashire Assizes which opened on Monday, 12 March 1866. However, in his opening address, Lush told the court he was disturbed to see that despite 'what was done by my learned brother Martin at the last Winter Assizes',[33] street robberies with violence had not been repressed. At the Winter Assizes Baron Martin had 23 garotters flogged. Lush was faced with 11 cases of robbery with violence most of whom had been committed within a fortnight of the Winter Assizes. None of this excited comment in the *Manchester Daily Examiner and Times*, the *Manchester Courier* and *Lancashire General Advertiser* or any other section of the press.

At the Winter Assizes of 1866 Baron Martin again presided and of 71 persons charged, 16 were charged with assault and robbery. 'There was little of special interest in the charge except the expressed intention of the learned judge to visit garotting cases with the heaviest punishment.' He declared that 'the streets of a city like this ought to be safe for people walking about at midnight as at noonday'. To achieve this end he handed down one sentence of 20 years penal servitude, five of 15 years and ten of seven years. Summing up he spoke in the past tense of 'Manchester, where robbery with violence, or, as it is called, garotting, prevailed to a degree scarcely to be believed'.[34]

It would appear that the Manchester outbreak of garotting of 1865–66 recalled by Bent was a reality involving some 50 convictions and, therefore, a lot of police activity, and yet it went unremarked by the City Council, the provincial or the national press. This outbreak came only two years after the Security from Violence Act, thus demonstrating the inadequacy of the Act, yet it excited no discussion. The fact that no comment was forthcoming implies that the press no longer considered garotting as newsworthy. It is notable that this provincial outbreak attracted no comment in the metropolitan press.

V

On Tuesday, 5 June 1867 *The Times* published seven letters all referring to separate attacks on passers-by by roughs who were accompanying bands of militia marching through the streets. The *Daily News* spoke of the roughs as the 'wolf' who had 'come without warning, found the shepherd sleeping and made havoc in the fold'.[35] It is impossible to believe that gangs of roughs suddenly decided that 3 June was the day to come out into the open and many of the correspondents' comments imply that it was common-place for any militia march to be accompanied by such a gang. One is forced to draw the conclusion that *The Times* had decided that the time was right to campaign against this phenomenon.

'F.M.W.' had his hat crushed and his umbrella broken by a 'body of fully 100 ruffianly thieves' whom he believed 'was not the ordinary larking crowd of roughs but a compact body of thieves, many with thick staves'. 'E.C.' had been strolling along Pall Mall East when he found himself in the middle of 'a crowd of roughs and pickpockets' who were accompanying a regiment of militia. One had tried to snatch his watch but he had broken his umbrella over the rough's head. 'W.R.H.' had been traversing Cavendish Square when he 'saw coming in the opposite direction ten or a dozen "roughs" of the worst type'. They assaulted the stout gentleman who was walking in front of him, stole his watch and picked all his pockets. 'W.R.H.' fled back to Regent Street. He attributed the presence of the roughs to a 'militia regiment hard by'. 'H.D.' had stopped in the Mall to let the Guards from the palace-yard pass when he was rushed 'by a whole posse of roughs'. He was robbed of his watch and chain and kicked in the shins, thigh and knee. He estimated the posse to 'number certainly not less than 50 men and boys'.

'W' was attacked on the New Road. What annoyed him was not the roughing up and the loss of his watch, scarf, pin, purse, handkerchief and umbrella but the attitude of onlookers. Having been attacked he went to a local shop to recover but the proprietor 'kindly invited me to walk out again, for fear I should collect a crowd around'. The whole occurrence was witnessed by several respectably dressed persons who merely watched 'apparently much amused'. 'G' was outside St Pancras Church in the Euston Road when he was 'surrounded by 16 or 20 blackguards from 15–25 years of age' who took his watch and the contents of his pockets. 'J.S.' had suffered a similar attack and felt it 'high time that the public should raise their voice and insist on the alteration of the laws'. 'J.S.' suggested corporal punishment or the sending of such roughs for long terms down the mines so they could be self-supporting.

This series of letters represents a classic cameo of folk devils and their ability to cause a panic. The inventory consisted of the keyword 'roughs' which implied a form of sub-human species. The blame lay with the militia who just looked on, the police who were not present and other members of respectable society who did nothing. The cry is then raised for a change in the control culture with an increase in police activity and a greater severity of punishment.

The main cause of the trouble was the march of the City of London Militia from Finsbury to Regent's Park. They were accompanied by 30 to 40 roughs, who according to *The Times* were mainly costermongers who stole an estimated 60 watches. The *Daily News* quoted the Home Secretary's statement in Parliament that they were an organised gang of thieves and that there were 26 robberies resulting in the loss of goods worth at least £150.[36] In reply to Owen Stanley's statement that, 'From what had appeared in the newspaper, it appeared that in some instances, the police, when appealed to, had refused to do their duty',[37] the Home Secretary stated that the police had not been notified of the intended march and so were understrength but had still managed to arrest 15 persons. The police, he said, were overburdened at the time with special duties. For example, between 300 and 400 police were on duty to protect the capital from the intrusion of the cattle plague.

The Times professed to be interested in the timing of the phenomenon although they did not comment on the possible influence of the press. The editor believed crimes were like crops and offences have their seasons but could never recall a more 'astonishing crop of outrages than has sprung up in this first week of June'. He believed that only ten days previously London streets were as safe as any in the country but were now 'so full of danger that it seems nobody could meet a small crowd even in broad daylight without being exposed to assault and robbery'.

The police were inevitably criticised. *The Illustrated London News* described the rampages of the 'unhuman class' and opined that the 'police were afraid to take vigorous measures for repression' although they believed that six stalwart constables bludgeoning without ruth or pause would have routed the mob and set them an example.[38] *The Times* published a satirical letter supposedly from an Italian bandit as a tilt at the police, in which the writer wonders why he ambushes travellers on lonely roads when passers-by can be relieved of the valuables 'by means of a flying column of brigands in the streets of a crowded city', ruefully adding that in Italy the authorities 'have not permitted us these distractions'.[39] The *Daily News* recommended that the police should make greater use of the telegraph to concentrate men in a hurry. 'E.C.' suggested that the police should march with the bands to the extent of their beat where the next patrolmen might take over. He added that, 'if this cannot be done, I should recommend Bob Wilson, the Sheriff of

Denver, the gentleman who shoots clean, to fill the situation of the Chief of Police'.[40] The appointment of Bob Wilson was unnecessary for, as with so many of the moral panics, the police took quiet and effective action. By the time the letter was published the police had received the following orders:

> *Militia or Volunteers on the March through the Streets* – If it be known in any Division that a Regiment or Militia or Volunteers is to march through the streets, arrangements are to be made to place constables, not less than two together, along the line, at as short distances from each other as practicable. The constables are to be taken from those on day duty in other parts of the Division, or from the night duty ... The Reserves not specifically assigned to other duties are also to be employed as above mentioned.[41]

Hence, at the departure of the Belgian Volunteers on Saturday, 20 July 1867, police of all ranks were on duty and the departure of the second contingent the following Monday was covered by 631 officers.[42]

One of the most important features of the 'outrages' of June 1867 was that, for the first time, the 'roughs' were folk devils. For the roughs theft was a secondary element compared to the fun of the assault. They were not professional thieves and as such were a difficult phenomenon for the middle classes to cope with. There was a certain understandable rationale to a garotter's actions and it could be presumed that his attack would cease if the victim handed over his valuables, but for the rough the satisfaction was gained from the embarrassment and humiliation of the victim. It will be seen later that the roughs were an ever-present problem throughout the second half of the nineteenth century but were to appear again in the newspapers as the Cornermen of Liverpool in 1874, the Liverpool High Rip gang in 1886 and in the aftermath of the Trafalgar Square riot of the same year.

The Daily News noted:

> This was the work neither of the London mob proper nor of scientific members of the furtive community; it was done by ruffians belonging undoubtedly to the criminal class, but to that rude and violent section of it whose numbers are practically unlimited. This is the most dangerous feature of the movement, London can turn out any day twenty-seven such gangs.

The immediate solution advocated was, unimaginatively, the 'cat'. 'The united press of London now calls on tribunals to put down these brutalities', declared the *Illustrated London News*, 'The Cat is the only missionary for the ruffian'.[43] The *Daily News* advised that, 'larger sentences should be meted out'. *The Times* counselled that, 'impunity breeds crime' while 'detection and punishment ... act with equal effect in checking its growth'. As garotting had disappeared with 'a few examples of condign retribution' it advised that 'a similar lesson cannot be too expeditiously administered in the case before us'.

It is unlikely that the cat would make the rough disappear. The rough was the unwanted but inevitable by-product of a social structure from which, on the whole, the middle-class newspaper readership benefited. Only a change in the social environment could possibly eliminate the rough. In the twentieth century the social environment has become more equable at the lower end of the social scale and yet the roughs still exist and many members of the middle classes still call for the return of the birch to deal with them. The press are still prone to highlight their existence from time to time, giving them new names (e.g. spivs, teddy-boys, mods, rockers, greasers, hell's angels, bovver boys, boot boys, skinheads, punks) in order to convince society that investigative journalism has 'discovered' a new sub-culture. One of the first of these named sub-cultures which the press 'discovered' was the Cornermen of Liverpool.

VI

On 11 August 1874 *The Times* printed a story which was copied directly from the *Spectator* and the *Liverpool Daily Post* concerning the death of Richard Morgan. Morgan, a married man of twenty-six, who worked as a shopman and 'of unusually good character' was walking down Tithebarn Street with his wife. The street was crowded. A gang of roughs led by a man called M'Grave asked him for sixpence. He refused and told them to 'work for their money, the same as he had to'. He was instantly knocked down, half-stunned, and when his brother went to his aid, he was disabled by savage kicks on the legs. Morgan's wife was violently pulled away from his prostrate body and he was kicked for ten minutes. When Morgan was later examined by a surgeon it was found that he had died of heart failure accelerated by the violence he had sustained.

The Tithebarn Street Murder, as it was called, provided the initial deviance for the London press to produce a new inventory in a year which it reviewed as 'comparatively uneventful'.[44] The inventory was a sustained attack on Lancashire in general and Liverpool in particular as being a uniquely brutalised area of Britain. The 'Cornermen' did not produce a real panic although they did constitute classic folk devils. This was mainly because 'Cornermen' were a provincial and not a metropolitan phenomenon and partly because they only preyed on their own class or kind. *The Times* report had noted that 'these roughs do not attack ladies. They would hesitate before attacking anyone in the dress which they identified with gentlemen'. The Liverpool press used the affair to voice their views on the Watch Committee while *The Times* concentrated on the slum city into which Liverpool was turning. The Home Secretary took prompt action to find out the facts as to whether crimes of brutality were on the increase, decided they were and introduced a bill to bring back flogging. The bill was quietly dropped two months later.

Five men were charged with Morgan's murder and appeared in court in December 1874. Three (M'Grave, Mullen and Campbell) were sentenced to death. The newspapers strongly expressed their wish to see the sentences carried out. Campbell, however, who had arrived after the fight had started, and probably after Morgan's death, was reprieved. The view of the *Daily Post* that his case, 'was probably one in which consideration was due to the merciful view taken of it by the jury' was not widely held. Most newspapers felt that justice had not been done. The *Liverpool Albion* stated that Campbell's reprieve was a mistake and would 'seriously impair the calculated warning intended to be conveyed by the fate of the other two'. After the hanging the *Daily Post* noted 'public sentiment could have accepted no other penalty',[45] while the *Spectator* was of the same opinion but felt that in the case of the reprieve the jury was at fault, not the Home Secretary.[46]

Cornermen were not a new phenomenon in the large cities. They were vicious, street-corner loafers who were glad of an excuse for a fight. Drink undoubtedly worsened their propensity to commit violence but was not a necessary concomitant. An ex-police sergeant maintained that cornermen had existed for years[47] and Edwin Chadwick noted in 1868 that in one week Exeter, Oxford, Teignmouth and Malton had all been at 'the mercy of rowdies'.[48] As early as 1862 Shimmin had described the 'genuine Liverpool Roughs'. In a Lombrosian fashion he noted these 'men of short stature, with big heads, broad, flat faces, and thick necks' who wore 'white trousers turned up at the bottom to show their high-laced, greasy boots'. According to Shimmin nothing could compare with their vulgarity, obscenity and impertinence.[49] A similar account appears thirteen years later in *The Porcupine* which in an earlier edition had defined cornermen as 'the ruffians who infest the corners of our Liverpool streets, and are ready for any deed of mischief and violence, from pitch and toss to manslaughter'.[50] The later account concludes that such people 'do not earn their livelihood by an honest labour, but do so by robbery, plunder and prostitution'.[51]

The symbol of the cornerman was his footwear. The author of 'The Ethics of Puncing', writing in the manuscript magazine *Odds and Ends* in 1881 refers to these as 'crusters' and advises that 'crusters take by far the largest share, if not at times the whole, of his affection'.[52] The author notes that an operative would wear clogs for work and would have an extra pair, more ornate 'coming to a long curled-up brass-capped point, and embellished with a profusion of brass-headed nails'. These were called 'duck bills'. A labourer would wear 'a great pair of heavy brass boots thickly studded with hob nails'. 'C.W.E.' describes the boot of the ironwork puddler which could be purchased at any shoemakers in iron and coal districts. It was 'covered over the whole sole with large iron nails, the heads shaped like the roof of a house, and raising the actual sole about half an inch from the ground. Sometimes, in substitution of nails, near the tip there is an iron plate'.[53] The need for such descriptions of working-class footwear aided the symbolism of the mythology whilst high-lighting how divorced were the majority of the population from the depredations of the cornermen. No one was alarmed, merely interested to learn how the wild tribes of Lancashire lived out their lives.

At the same time that cornermen were in the headlines the public's attention was directed to another Lancashire phenomenon dependent upon the boot. This was brutal wife-beating. Along with Morgan's murderers was hanged a man who had kicked his wife to death. Following an argument in the street he kicked her in the ribs until she bled. A policeman arrived and advised them to return home and settle their quarrel. Having slept off the ill effects of alcohol the man saw the error of his ways. He proceeded to kick his wife again but this time also beat her about the head with a poker.[54] Preceding the trial of Morgan's murderers a particularly gruesome case heard at Manchester Assizes on 10 December 1874 received wide publicity and did little to enhance the Lancashire image. This motiveless crime involved five colliers, aged twenty-one to twenty-six, throwing a brick through the window of a seventy-four year-old Irishman's cottage two miles outside St Helens. The men demanded entry, smashed down the door and threw quick-lime in the face of the man's wife who went to seek the aid of the police. Meanwhile the man was struck in the eye 'with such violence that the eyeball was completely smashed and the contents of the eye poured out'. The men, knowing they were recognised, 'filled up his wounded eye with quick-lime: they crammed lime up his nostrils, forced it down his throat, and left him on his bed for dead'.[55]

The criminal statistics (see Tables 4.6 – 4.8) show that violent crime was rife in Lancashire in 1874 but not more so than in certain other years. Nor was violence a uniquely Lancastrian problem. However, the

Table 4.6 Committals for the indictable offence of assault and inflicting bodily harm 1860–1880

	1860	1861	1862	1863	1864	1865	1866
England and Wales	209	?	191	281	306	293	272
Liverpool Borough	52	42	39	95	101	89	91
Manchester City	17	18	7	14	17	10	3
Metropolitan Police District	–	3	2	1	2	1	35

	1867	1868	1869	1870	1871	1872	1873
England and Wales	295	409	395	362	314	300	381
Liverpool Borough	99	199	101	118	76	107	164
Manchester City	10	19	21	17	21	19	25
Metropolitan Police District	10	24	41	31	24	42	43

	1874	1875	1876	1877	1878	1879	1880
England and Wales	424	575	607	447	348	263	374
Liverpool Borough	120	156	40	79	61	46	?
Manchester City	20	22	50	4	8	6	6
Metropolitan Police District	39	50	50	78	49	?	64

Sources: *Judicial Statistics*, P.P. 1860–1880

Table 4.7 Committals for the indictable offence of assaults, common, 1860–1880

	1860	1861	1862	1863	1864	1865	1866
England and Wales	146	?	128	163	214	229	217
Liverpool Borough	–	–	11	13	15	5	4
Manchester City	22	31	47	12	8	3	1
Metropolitan Police District	54	68	54	74	143	150	156

	1867	1868	1869	1870	1871	1872	1873
England and Wales	190	165	188	156	124	128	99
Liverpool Borough	4	11	12	3	–	1	3
Manchester City	–	1	1	1	1	1	2
Metropolitan Police District	125	109	127	115	89	88	71

	1874	1875	1876	1877	1878	1879	1880
England and Wales	144	172	114	129	167	115	186
Liverpool Borough	15	24	7	9	3	2	7
Manchester City	5	–	8	–	–	2	1
Metropolitan Police District	89	108	77	83	107	?	147

Sources: As Table 4.6

Table 4.8 Committals for the indictable offence of robbery on the highway 1860–1880

	1860	1861	1862	1863	1864	1865	1866
England and Wales	501	?	497	620	627	633	680
Liverpool Borough	55	6	–	11	57	46	56
Manchester City	82	119	128	144	132	195	217
Metropolitan Police District	30	38	63	115	78	97	101
	1867*	1868	1869	1870	1871	1872	1873
England and Wales	691	703	612	563	452	453	439
Liverpool Borough	94	52	123	73	38	44	77
Manchester City	201	202	142	100	40	33	45
Metropolitan Police District	119	90	119	121	74	66	47
	1874	1875	1876	1877	1878	1879	1880
England and Wales	511	558	491	465	385	449	417
Liverpool Borough	90	116	104	102	97	72	44
Manchester City	52	?	48	46	51	45	45
Metropolitan Police District	48	40	71	59	?(160)	101	96

Sources: As Table 4.6
* N.B. From 1867 the offence was defined as 'Robbery'.

reporting of violence in 1874 in the press seems to have been uniquely Lancastrian to the exclusion of other areas. A certain mythology was created stereotyping Lancastrians as brutal on a par with the stereotyping of Scottish miserliness and Irish stupidity.

Table 4.6 shows that there was a large number of indictable assaults (120) in Liverpool in 1874 but that this figure represented a 26.8 per cent decrease on the previous year's figure. Why had there not been a flurry of press comment in 1873? In conjunction with Table 4.10 it can be demonstrated that different areas used different levels of justice in different ways and with differing emphasis. It would seem, for example, that Manchester magistrates were more keen (or perhaps felt more confident) to deal with cases of assault summarily whereas Liverpool magistrates were more prone to send such cases involving bodily harm to a higher court. Similarly, metropolitan magistrates were not averse to dealing with common assaults as an indictable offence (see Table 4.7) whereas this was clearly not the case in Liverpool and Manchester. The Chief Constable's report for the year ending September 1875 drew attention to 'the fact that in Liverpool, no person booked for any offence can be discharged till he appears before a magistrate. This practice is not

Table 4.9 Summary committals for assaults, aggravated, on women and children, 1860–1880

	1860	1861	1862	1863	1864	1865	1866
England and Wales	2,943	2,985	2,859	3,044	3,202	3,100	3,047
Liverpool Borough	188	197	159	170	198	200	204
Manchester City	27	18	24	15	31	75	99
Metropolitan Police District	?	652	551	508	427	358	326

	1867	1868	1869	1870	1871	1872	1873
England and Wales	2,623	?	2,702	2,571	2,727	?	2,713
Liverpool Borough	210	168	164	177	125	90	?
Manchester City	70	64	76	61	81	66	38
Metropolitan Police District	192	160	191	295	289	271	326

	1874	1875	1876	1877	1878	1879	1880
England and Wales	2,841	3,166	2,737	2,687	2,556	2,229	2,091
Liverpool Borough	82	110	100	73	64	55	60
Manchester City	101	104	?	82	76	44	44
Metropolitan Police District	301	341	313	368	346	217	209

Sources: As Table 4.6

Table 4.10 Summary committals for assaults, 1860–1880

	1860	1861	1862	1863	1864	1865	1866
England and Wales	62,748	62,498	64,385	70,533	77,726	81,842	77,640
Liverpool Borough	1,551	1,758	1,842	1,707	1,865	1,819	1,649
Manchester City	1,417	1,664	1,803	1,607	?	1,857	1,938
Metropolitan Police District	?	13,352	13,529	14,484	16,442	17,716	17,199

	1867	1868	1869	1870	1871	1872	1873
England and Wales	74,980	77,112	77,864	74,985	77,224	80,650	79,788
Liverpool Borough	1,628	1,537	1,542	1,461	1,372	1,802	1,849
Manchester City	1,782	1,842	?	2,128	1,920	1,944	2,028
Metropolitan Police District	17,004	15,978	16,721	15,210	15,128	16,294	15,937

	1874	1875	1876	1877	1878	1879	1880
England and Wales	85,676	?	83,104	78,050	74,630	66,395	68,888
Liverpool Borough	1,427	1,413	1,323	1,227	1,174	1,145	1,062
Manchester City	2,084	2,066	2,013	1,832	1,770	1,739	1,448
Metropolitan Police District	16,355	16,226	16,848	?	17,420	?	17,061

Sources: as Table 4.6

carried out in other towns'. To support his claim he cites the example of 'a seaport similar to Liverpool', whose recorded numbers of drunkenness were 8,345 (compared to Liverpool's 20,330) but the Chief Constable's report for that city discloses that 22,261 persons drunk and incapable were discharged by the officer on duty and not enumerated.[56] This was just another example of statistics saying little about reality. However, even treating the statistics themselves as facts, the timing and subject of the 1874 press outburst against Liverpool was illogical. Table 4.8 shows that it was robbery that was on the increase in Liverpool rather than assault and that if assaults on women are considered (See Table 4.9) then the Liverpool figures were the lowest they had been since 1860. 1874 and 1875 were not particularly the years of the brute in Liverpool but merely the years that the press focused attention on an ever-present problem. The Tithebarn Street murder, as an initial deviance, was not particularly remarkable considering that convictions for murder in the whole of England and Wales were greater in 1875 than for any previously recorded year.

However unfair the focusing of press attention on Lancashire (and Liverpool in particular) two facts remain. First, that the attention was focused there, and secondly, that in 1874 there was a total of 507 cases of brutal assault dealt with in Lancashire, second only to the 742 in the far more densely populated metropolis.

VII

In the mid-1880s the Liverpool newspapers revealed a new cause for alarm which was referred to as the 'High Rip Gang', which the Chief Constable, William Nott-Bower, was later to refer to as 'an invention which seemed to take the fancy of the press'.[57] They were first mentioned by Mr Justice Butt in an address to the Grand Jury at the Winter Assize of 1884. Following the murder of a Spanish sailor in Blackstock Street, he said that the murderer, M'lean, 'was the leader of the "High Rip Gang"; he had a great deal to do with its organisation, and during his life the district was a veritable Alsatia',[58] The existence of the High Rips as an entity was very much in dispute and it was this dispute which formed the central theme of the whole affair.

The *Liverpool Echo* which was convinced that 'there is as much intimidation and terrorism in the portion of the city lying between Scotland Road and the river as there is in the most disturbed district in Ireland', stated quite categorically that, 'the most important point, however, in this matter is the question as to whether or not there is any organisation amongst the young ruffians'.[59]

The central event which gave justification to the newspaper publicity was a march on Walton Gaol on 4 September 1886 by 150 youths. Following a dispute between the 'Logwood' and the 'High Rip' a man was stabbed to death and there was a 'sensation in court' when the two nineteen year-olds responsible were sentenced to fifteen years penal servitude each. The youths gathered at the gaol to meet a young man who had been a witness for the prosecution at the petty sessions and kicked him to death. This, in newspaper terminology, was twisted from an 'Attack at Walton Gaol' to 'The Attack on Walton Gaol'.

The High Rip episode lasted from late August 1886 until mid-November and reached its climax in October. The dates are important, for, with the benefit of hindsight, the cynical observer may be forgiven for feeling that while 'Savage Liverpool', 'The High Rip: Is it a secret society?', and 'Does High Rip Exist?' are all important questions of the day, the main issue was the holding of municipal elections on 1 November 1886. The conclusion was that the Conservatives increased their hold on the council over the Liberals from 42–22 to 47–17.[60] This was a vindication of the Watch Committee and the Chief Constable who noted that the newspaper publicity 'created considerable and entirely justifiable alarm, though there was never the very faintest shadow of foundation for the suggestions made'.[61]

The main contributors to the controversy were the *Liverpool Daily Post*, which had the highest circulation of any morning newspaper in the city and employed a special commissioner to uncover the High Rip, the *Liverpool Echo* which had the highest evening circulation and supported the *Post*'s attacks on the Watch Committee and the *Liverpool Review* which supported the establishment. The episode is of especial interest for several reasons. It demonstrates how newspapers decided the precise point in time that an issue was an issue. The *Daily Post* stated that, 'For some two or three years this gang of thieves have made themselves notorious by the frequence and violence of their depredation',[62] but made no apology for not having brought it to the attention of its readers earlier. It shows the newspapers' method of stating a viewpoint and then only reporting facts which support that viewpoint. The episode also provides material which casts light upon the myths, half-truths and perhaps even some facts with which the reader was confronted and which would have shaped the newspaper reader's perception of life in Liverpool.

On 26 August 1886, whilst complaining about further increases in the numbers of police, the *Liverpool Daily Post* observed that 'there is nothing in the social or moral condition of Liverpool to compare unfavourably with other centres of population'. Exactly nine days later the same newspaper was writing of 'the existence of this life of savagery, running parallel with the ordinary life of refinement and high civilisation'.

The *Daily Post*, remarkably out of touch with events, noted that the phrase 'Cornermen' to describe the ruffians 'is of recent origin; though it is so widely known locally as almost to be classic'. The *Liverpool Review* took a different view. Recent assaults and outrages had led people to believe that, 'the old-established Cornermen had suddenly broken through the bound which had kept them in some measure under control' but the High Rip was not a combination of Cornermen. It was this and something more. 'It was the union of some of the worst elements of this class with the worst type of hobbledehoy'.[63] According to the *Review* the 'hobbledehoy' differed from the 'professional cornermen' in that the former did sometimes engage in honest labour. The *Review* then proceeded to provide a classic example of journalistic hypocrisy. Four weeks later as the election drew nearer and the Watch Committee and Town Council were facing increasing criticism from the press, the newspaper that had devoted a column to defining High Rip, and complaining of its existence in the Islington district, turned volte-face. The *Review* prefaced an interview with a police official with the warning that before the actions of the High Rip could be stopped 'it must be established that the nefarious organisation has any existence', upon which matter the *Review* would 'not at present offer an opinion'.[64]

Whether operating as a cohesive gang or not the newspapers were agreed that the perpetrators of street violence in Liverpool were youths between seventeen and twenty-two years old, hailing from the north end of the city 'which it is dangerous to enter after dark, and which the police traverse in couples'.[65] It was generally acknowledged that the youths were either unemployed or took the most lucrative unskilled job on the docks of scaling boilers or steamers. Their *modus operandi* was in dispute. The *Review* viewed them as congregations of roughs whose favourite pastime was making ribald comments at and jostling young women or crushing the hats of passers-by. If there was any retaliation the victim would be attacked.[66] It was the opinion of the police, stated in an interview with the *Review* that many passers-by brought trouble on themselves by making comments at gangs of youths as 'there are lots of men who believe themselves "able" for a score, and plunge into a row for the sheer love of the thing. Of course they get the worst of it'.[67] The *Daily Post* commissioner believed, however, that the former gang systematically levied blackmail on dock labourers and knew how much each man had worked each week and what he could afford to pay. He found 'the cruellest feature of the case is that people whom they rob are poor people, who can least afford to lose their money'.[68] It is true that the High Rip's victims were from the lower socio-economic groups and this most certainly explains the lack of interest shown in the episode by the national press and the government. Although the quality of the attacks were in dispute the quantity was not. The newspapers all seemed to accept the validity of the figures supplied by 'One who knows' that the North Dispensary treated, on average, one hundred persons per week for assault wounds.[69]

Views on the history of the phenomenon ranged from those who believed it did not exist to those who believed that street violence of this type had always been present. Both extremes made the whole affair unnewsworthy. What was required was a novelty aspect. At first the *Daily Post* introduced a sense of history by portraying the gang as a phoenix rising from the ashes. They recalled a similar type of gang, the 'Hibernians' in the 1860s which had no organisation, but met at wakes or on street corners, in public houses or in empty houses and planned robberies.[70] No one else recalled them. Then the intrepid *Daily Post* commissioner went 'protected by the accompaniment of an employer' into the hunting ground of the High Rip. He found they wore 'bucko' hats and signalled to each other by means of three shrill whistles. They carried knives ('bleeders') but their most formidable weapon was a belt with several sharpened buckles which could inflict wounds indistingui- shable from knife wounds at a range of four feet. The commissioner found a reformed High Rip who told of the secret society basis of the organisation and described the initiation ceremony which consisted of cutting the wrist with a knife and swearing never to attack a person without drawing blood and allegiance to other gang members.[71]

This was folk-devil mythology taken to the limit and one sympathises with 'J.C.'s' assessment of the situation as an 'absurd fiction, which at present is going the rounds of the press',[72] and with that of the police, who to the comment that the High Rip had created a scare, replied 'Thanks to you gentlemen of the press ... it is you who have produced it'.[73]

Although the High Rip seemed to retain the limelight it was stated that there were three other gangs in existence – the 'Logwood', 'Finon Hadie' and the 'Dead Rabbit'. The *Daily Post* commissioner produced more inside information on the 'Logwood' against some of whose members several warrants had been issued for riotous assembly. He believed they were, 'in reality a sort of vigilance committee, being formed of working men who have banded themselves together to put an end to the High Rip Gang'. Their alleged *modus operandi* was to capture members of the High Rip and force them to go down on their knees and vow to work. The *Daily Post*, of course, agreed that such lynch law could not be tolerated but found it 'at least gratifying' that there was an organisation amongst the people dedicated to stopping the depredations of the High Rip.

The idea of fighting like with like and forming a vigilante gang appealed to many correspondents. 'M' suggested that if the Watch Committee was incapable of controlling the situation then a meeting of the citizens should be called to agree on what should be done.[74] 'A Citizen' suggested the use of plain clothes gangs[75] while the *Daily Post* recommended 'a strong patrol of police, armed with the sticks carried by sergeants, passing through the district at irregular times'. The other remedy recommended was, of course, the cat.

The *Liverpool Review* brought the episode to a fitting close on 5 March 1887 with the conclusion that:

> We have always regarded the stories of High Rip Outrages as somewhat mythical, at any rate to the extent that we believed them to be worked up to a point of serious exageration for sensational poster purposes.

The High Rip seems a clear case of newspapers suddenly focusing on an existing situation of street violence in low neighbourhoods. By attributing all crimes of violence to an organised street society they created the kind of scare which had the double benefit of boosting newspaper sales and of embarrassing the establishment. As is shown in a later chapter, the establishment had long been aware of the real problem and had been coping with it to the best of their ability.

VIII

A similar phenomenon to the High Rip which was not given publicity in the press were the scuttlers. These were rival gangs in the lower parts of Manchester and Salford. Their existence is mentioned in the autobiographies of two Manchester police officers and the work of C.E.B. Russell and formed the subject of a book by Alex Devine.[76] In a recent work Geoffrey Pearson has noted that 'they were such a force that the public authorities made various petitions to the Home Secretary for sterner measures to put them down'.[77] However, they receive no mention in the Manchester Chief Constable's reports, except for that of 1886 when it is noted that against a background of 'a diminution in almost all classes of offence' there had been 'a slight increase in the number of juveniles under sixteen years arrested'.[78] The magistrates did seem to react with the birch. In 1886, 935 such juveniles were arrested (an increase of 70 over 1885) of which 86 were birched. In 1887 of 910, 114 were birched and by 1889 the number arrested had dropped to 753 but the number birched rose to 138.[79]

Jerome Caminada, ex-Chief Detective Inspector of Manchester police, relates a fight between the Clock Alley lads and the Greengate gang in 1868 and admits that, although he had met all kinds of desperate thieves, he 'would rather face the worst of these than a scuttler' as he 'relies on the free use of the knife for maintaining his position'.[80] James Bent said the gangs numbered as many as fifty youths carrying sticks, stones, bricks and knives, although 'their favourite instrument of violence is a strong leather belt'.[81] Russell said the gangs were twenty to thirty strong and were armed with heavily buckled belts and mineral water bottles. Writing in 1891 Bent said that 'not very long ago' a medical man had told him that 'scarcely a day passed' without Manchester Infirmary having to treat someone brought in as a result of a scuttling affray.

Bent believed that the scuttlers were a purely Manchunian product and were unknown in other parts of the country. He was obviously untravelled and had not come across the Liverpool Cornermen, the Peaky Blinders of Birmingham, the Hooligans of London and all the other dialect names for the rough gangs which inhabited every major city. Despite Russell's advice that the best remedy was 'above all, refuse to ignore the fact of their existence',[82] these major gang fights between lower-class groups caused the newspapers no disquiet. Such disinterest must inevitably be concluded to have been a function of the small number of middle-class residents in the lower parts of Manchester, Salford, Miles Platting, Gorton, Beswick and Openshaw. It was probably also a result of familiarity. David Jones states that throughout the 1850s and 1860s in Manchester police division A, gangs of youths often attacked pedestrians and robbed them. The average take was £3. In the early 1850s pedestrians were often knocked unconscious, half-strangled and smothered with a chloroform pad.[83] In 1840 W.B. Neale had described juvenile delinquents in Manchester 'hanging in groups about the corners of streets ... and others again in small knots, concocting some new robbery'.[84]

IX

Perhaps the metropolitan press ignored the problems of the provincial cities and their High Rips and Scuttlers in 1886 because of the problems posed by the roughs in early 1886 in the capital itself. G.M. Young observes in that year, 'the nerves of the capital were put to the test and found wanting', for in February of that year the East End met the West End and 'before the police recovered control of the situation the attendant roughs had helped themselves, it was rumoured, to some £50,000 of shopkeepers' goods'.[85]

The Trafalgar Square demonstration and the trouble which followed it was and is seen by many as being of a political nature. The rising socialists were thought to be converting the disenchanted unemployed and inciting them to revolution. Asa Brigs believes that the riots were a result of 'animosities against the propertied and privileged people in London' and notes that many Victorians felt the same, as contributions to the Lord Mayor's Relief Fund increased from £3,000 to £80,000 in forty-eight hours.[86] In 1870 the *Quarterly Review* drew on the experience of the Hyde Park Riot of 1868 to make observations on the role of the roughs in such 'political' demonstrations. The 1868 riot had been the only occasion since the formation of the Metropolitan Police in 1829 that the police had called on military force to aid them in quelling a mob. On this occasion 'the roughs and thieves turned out in overwhelming force' and it had long been acknowledged that 'there is never any difficulty experienced in summoning a large crowd of the idle and desperate classes of the metropolis', and that any reform meeting would be attended by some genuine reformers and 'in still greater numbers the roughs and the dregs of the roughs'. The author issued the salutary warning that:

> The security of London consists in keeping these roughs apart, and the danger of London consists in concentrating them in mass where they feel sufficiently strong to pick pockets, smash windows, pull down railings or stone the police with comparative impunity'.[87]

Although the original demonstration was organised by a political body representing the unemployed and labouring classes and many of those who read the newspaper reports the next day feared the socialist spectre and thought it appropriate to counter socialism with charity, the actual trouble was not politically motivated. The motive was hinted at following an earlier riot resulting from the Sunday Trading Bill demonstration in Hyde Park in July 1855. The police had issued a notification banning the demonstration and this 'held out to the populace, beside the pleasure of annoying the well-dressed, the further gratification of a skirmish with the police'.[88] The pool of unemployed roughs was vast in 1886 and street violence was still common. The

Liverpool Echo wrote with relief that 'the epidemic of street ruffiansim is not confined to Liverpool alone. In the Metropolis charges of street violence are more rife at the present time than they have been for some years past'.[89] The statistics support this assertion. In February 1886 23 cases of robbery appeared before the London courts (see Fig. 2.1) compared to 7 in Liverpool. For the whole of 1885 and 1886 London courts dealt with 82 and 84 cases of robbery respectively, the corresponding figures for Liverpool being 17 and 26.

Trafalgar Square was regarded by many as the finest site in Europe. The approaches to the square were in a state of change. Northumberland Avenue was built and opened in 1876. Shaftesbury Avenue which had taken eight years to build, cutting, as it did, through the St Giles rookery, was about to be opened in 1886. Owing to traffic congestion a new road was being built from Tottenham Court Road to Trafalgar Square, called Charing Cross Road, which would be opened in 1887.[90] The square itself was as it looks today.

A rally of unemployed persons was called for Monday, 8 February 1886 by the London Workmen's Committee. This organisation was separate from the Social Democratic Federation which was the most influential of the London socialist organisations. Its tactics were based on the theory that the metropolis should lead the country and it believed that the failure of Chartism had been its inability to mobilise the metropolis. In 1887, its leader, Henry Hyndman, was to write a pamphlet, *A Commune for Socialism*, calling for municipal socialism. On 5 February notices appeared in newspapers describing the socialist meeting which called on London socialists to attend the gathering and urging them to seize the platform of the Working Men's Committee. A crowd of between twenty and thirty thousand gathered in the square. The sympathetic *Reynolds' Weekly* considered that it consisted of 'chiefly building trades and dock workers' and that although the occasion was used by the revolutionary Social Democratic Federation to give speeches, the right-wing Fair Trade League had also sent speakers.[91] The *Morning Post* produced a more right-wing analysis of 'the disgraceful mob ... composed of a few fanatics, a great amount of loafers and idlers, and a huge contingent of professional thieves'.[92] According to the evidence of the police, 'there was in the crowd a considerable portion, larger than usual, of the roughest element'.[93] The meeting passed off in an orderly manner. Afterwards, however, gangs of roughs 'marched eastwards and westwards in a riotous manner, assaulting inoffensive pedestrians and causing considerable damage to property by stone-throwing'.[94] About 4 p.m. a portion of the mob, estimated by *Reynolds' Weekly* to number between one and two thousand, by the police as three to five thousand, drifted westward towards Pall Mall. Windows were broken at the Carlton Club (the recognised headquarters of the Conservatives) and all down St James's, Piccadilly. They smashed the windows of all the famous clubs in Pall Mall and looted many of the shops.

A socialist sympathiser saw the cause of the riot as the political awareness of the unemployed and the taunts by the members of the Reform Club and Carlton Club as the procession passed by.[95] In the heat of the moment the *Daily News* stated that, 'the riot was the direct consequence of the appeals made by the leaders of the Social Democratic Federation to the excited mob'. The following day, when emotion ran less high, the editor realised, 'it was no social revolution which broke the windows in Pall Mall ... it was mainly a rising of mere savagery and love of mischief' and that its main feature was not the presence of socialists but the 'predominance of mere roughs'.[96]

Hyndman and his compatriots were arrested and sent by Bow Street magistrates to the Central Criminal Court charged with inciting the mob. Before Mr Justice Cave, the jury without hesitation acquitted all of the accused. The establishment had realised that this was not the result of a political demonstration but merely another example of the London roughs seizing their opportunity of having a good time at middle-class expense. It provided a fine example of an initial deviance on which the press could seize resulting in a parliamentary committee on police conduct during the affair. The *Annual Register* made the telling observation that Parliament was not sitting at the time, having adjourned to allow the re-election of a new Cabinet, so that, 'public feeling had to make itself known through the press, with the necessary result of being unchecked by any sense of responsibility'.

X

These were the initial deviances of street violence in the nineteenth century. Some never led to the development of a nationally accepted inventory or on to the process of sensitisation, either because they did not affect the influential middle class or the influential metropolis; or simply because there were more newsworthy events happening at the same time. Others had effects which were more wide-reaching. Their reporting led to an over-estimation of the deviance and an escalation in the control culture. They attained the level of moral panics and the organisational culprits as well as the actual deviants felt the pressure for change. The street violence of the nineteenth century was, at times, seen to reflect the inefficiency of the police, prison and legal systems, which was in itself viewed by the public, under the guidance of the press, as a national scandal.

These initial deviances have no common characteristic save that the press chose to make them initial deviances. They can all be explained quite logically if seen as discrete events but when placed in the whole social environment of the nineteenth century their totally arbitrary nature is revealed. The panic of 1862 can be justified by an attack on a member of parliament and by rising robbery statistics. Yet, in the late 1870s Chief Baron Kelly, a privy councillor, was attacked on a foggy night by two garotters at the Tyburn Stone near Marble Arch. Kelly had put his back to the railings and fought them off with a stick until help arrived.[97] Surely this was the stuff of which good copy was made: a high court judge attacked in a major London thoroughfare. Tables 4.7 and 4.8 reveal that indictable assault cases were at a twenty-year high and robbery figures were rising at this time. Yet there was no outcry from the fourth estate. The panic of 1862–6 was justified by the number of robberies in the metropolis but table 4.8 reveals much higher figures in 1867, 1869 and 1870.

The 1874 Cornermen episode was the result of a youth gang killing a citizen and provided the metropolitan press with the ammunition to attack Liverpool. In 1886, the High Rip, a similar gang, kicked a prosecution witness to death outside Walton gaol and excited no comment in the metropolitan press. The High Rip kept the Liverpool press in copy for many months but the scuttlers failed to rouse the Manchester press. Such is the arbitrary nature of news selection.

It would be gratifying to be able to identify a clear guiding rule which editors followed when identifying an initial deviance but it is impossible to do so. The political views of the editor, the commercial influences of having to sell newspapers and attract advertising revenue, the competing copy available, were all influences. The identification of an initial deviance was probably not a conscious act. Moral panics were like Topsy – they just grew. The initial deviance was the bait. If the public and the politicians took the bait then the editor would produce more copy and keep reeling in the attention of his readership until either the line snapped and the readership lost interest or the catch was made and public pressure forced a change in the control culture. It is to the sensitisation, over-estimation and escalation of the control-culture aspects of Cohen's model in the successful moral panics of the nineteenth century that our attention is now directed.

Notes

1. A. Andrews, *The History of British Journalism*, (1859), Vol. 2, 347.
2. *Morning Post*, 14 December, 1859.
3. W. Hindle, *The Morning Post 1772–1937: Portrait of a Newspaper* (1937), 208.
4. *The Times*, 13 December 1851.
5. Letter from 'A Sufferer', *The Times*, 17 July 1851.
6. Letter crom 'A Victim of Thuggee', *The Times*, 19 July 1851.
7. W.L. Clay, *The Prison Chaplain* (1861), 443.
8. *The Times*, 28 May, 1852.
9. *The Times*, 8 October 1852.
10. *The Times*, 9 November 1852.
11. *The Times*, 28 November 1856.
12. *Globe*, 27 November 1856 reprinted *The Times*, 28 November 1856.
13. Letter from 'Rus in urbe', *The Times*, 23 December 1856.
14. R. and F. Davenport-Hill, *A Memoir of Matthew Davenport-Hill*, (1878), 201.
15. *Illustrated London News*, 29 November 1862.
16. *Shoreditch Advertiser*, 6 December 1862.
17. *Weekly Dispatch*, 17 August 1862.
18. Letter from 'Northumbrian', *Reynolds' Newspaper*, 7 December 1862.
19. *The Times*, 18 July 1862. Also *Weekly Dispatch*, 20 July 1862.
20. As with Table 4.2, the statistical year starts from the winter quarter of the previous year so that the 1863 figure includes the last quarter of 1862.
21. *Judicial Statistics*, 1863; *P.P., 1864, LVII*, 445 p.xi.
22. Ibid., pp. xii, xiii, xvi.
23. *Daily News*, 18 July 1862.
24. 'The ticket-of-leave system', *Quarterly Review*, 113 (1863), 139–175.
25. *The Times*, 5 December 1862.
26. *All the Year Round*, 6 December 1862.
27. *Daily News*, 4 December 1862.
28. *Shoreditch Advertiser*, 6 December 1862.
29. House of Lords report, *The Times*, 10 June 1863.
30. Letter from 'A chairman of quarter sessions', *The Times*, 6 December 1862.
31. *The Times*, 10 June, 1863.
32. W. Bent, *Criminal Life: Reminiscences of Forty-two Years as a Police Officer*, (1891), 220.
33. *Manchester Courier and Lancashire General Advertiser*, 13 March 1866.
34. *Manchester Examiner and Times*, 6 and 12 December 1866.
35. *Daily News*, 7 June, 1867.
36. *The Times*, 6 June, 1867. *Daily News*, 7 June 1867.
37. *Hansard*, 6 June 1867, 1665.
38. *Illustrated London News*, 15 June 1867.
39. Letter from 'Fru Diavolo', *The Times*, 6 June 1867.
40. Letter from 'E.C.', *The Times*, 5 June 1867. P.R.O. Me Pol 7/29.
41. *Metropolitan Police Orders*, 6 June 1867. P.R.O. Me Pol 7/29.
42. *Metropolitan Police Orders*, 20 July 1867. P.R.O. Me Pol 7/29.

43. *Illustrated Evening News*, 15 June 1867.
44. *The Times*, 31 December 1874.
45. *Daily Post*, 5 January 1875.
46. *Spectator*, 16 January 1875.
47. Letter from Ex Police Serjeant, *Daily Post*, 18 January 1875.
48. E. Chadwick, 'On the consolidation of the Police Force and the prevention of crime', *Fraser's Magazine*, LXXVII (1868), 12.
49. H. Shimmin, *Liverpool Sketches*, (1862), 122.
50. 'A caution to cornermen', *The Porcupine*, 19 December, 1874.
51. 'Considerations for cornermen', *The Porcupine*, 9 January 1875.
52. H.W. Whitcombe, 'The Ethics of Puncing', *Odds and Ends*, published by St Paul's Literary and Educational Society, Manchester (1881). Held by Manchester Public Libraries ref. M38/4/2/27.
53. Letter from 'C.W.E.', *Spectator*, 15 August 1874.
54. *The Times*, 5 January 1875.
55. *The Times*, 14 December 1874.
56. Report of the Police Establishment to the Watch Committee for the Borough of Liverpool 1875. Liverpool Records Office ref. H352.2 WAT.
57. Sir William Nott-Bower, *Fifty-two years a Policeman*, (1926), 145.
58. *Liverpool Daily Post*, 4 September 1886.
59. *Liverpool Echo*, 2 October 1886.
60. For the press to use criminal acts as election issues is equally common in the twentiety century. The *Daily Telegraph* editorial, 22 January 1982 noted that, 'Rape, of course, is suddenly everywhere in the newspapers and on television. The courts are thick with maligned women and brutal magistrates'. It noted that this was not because the number of rapes were increasing as sexual offences were at a ten-year low, but because the denunciation of magistrates showing leniency to rapists was a vote-catcher.
61. Nott-Bower, op.cit.
62. *Liverpool Daily Post*, 4 September 1886.
63. *Liverpool Review*, 28 August 1886.
64. *Liverpool Review*, 25 September 1886.
65. *Liverpool Daily Post*, 4 September 1886.
66. *Liverpool Review*, 28 August 1886.
67. *Liverpool Review*, 25 September 1886.
68. *Liverpool Daily Post*, 20 September 1886.
69. Letter from 'One who knows', *Liverpool Echo*, 14 October 1886.
70. *Liverpool Daily Post*, 4 September 1886.
71. *Liverpool Daily Post*, 20 September 1886 and reprinted in *Liverpool Echo*, 21 October 1886.
72. Letter from 'J.C.', *Liverpool Echo*, 21 October 1886.
73. *Liverpool Review*, 25 September 1886.
74. Letter from 'M', *Liverpool Echo*, 15 October 1886.
75. Letter from 'A Citizen', *Liverpool Echo*, 21 October 1886.
76. J. Bent, *Criminal Life: Reminiscences of Forty-two Years as a Police Officer*, (1891) 223; J. Caminada, *Twenty-five Years of Detective Life* (1895); C.E.B. Russell,

Manchester Boys: Sketches of Manchester Lads at Work and Play, (1905); A Devine, *Scuttlers and Scuttling* (1890).

77. G. Pearson, *Hooligan: A History of Respectable Fears* (1983), 94–98.
78. *Criminal and Miscellaneous Statistical Returns of the Manchester Police for the Year ended 29th September 1886*, Manchester Local History Library, 352.2 ML.
79. Ibid., 1887 and 1889.
80. Caminada, op.cit., 405.
81. Bent, op.cit., 224.
82. Russell, op.cit.
83. D. Jones, *Crime, Protest, Community and Police in Nineteenth-Century Britain*, (1982), 159.
84. W.B. Neale, *Juvenile Delinquency in Manchester: Its Causes and History, Its Consequences, and some Suggestions concerning its Cure* (1840).
85. G.M. Young, *Portrait of an Age*, (1936 reprinted 1960), 167.
86. A. Briggs, *Victorian Cities* (1963), 329.
87. 'The Police of London', *Quarterly Review*, 129 (1870).
88. *Annual Register* (1885).
89. *Liverpool Echo*, 22 September 1886.
90. G. Norton, *Victorian London* (1969), 77–79.
91. *Reynolds' Weekly Newspaper*, 14 February 1886.
92. *Morning Post*, 9 February 1886.
93. Disturbances (Metropolis): Report from the Committee on the Recent Disturbances and the Conduct of the Police Authorities, *P.P. (1886)*, c. 4665, XXXIV, III.
94. *Daily News*, 9 February 1886.
95. Letter from 'Northumbria', *Reynolds' Weekly Newspaper*, 14 February 1886.
96. *Daily News*, 10 February 1886.
97. W. Foulkes (Their Reporter), *A Generation of Judges*, (1886), 46.

5. The Effect of the Panics on the Middle Classes

I

This chapter attempts to consider how respectable middle-class opinion viewed these outbreaks of street violence or perceived street violence. Roger Lane has observed that 'the degree of public concern has never been, nor is now, an accurate index of the degree of criminal activity. Indeed, the reverse is often true'.[1] However, as has been argued previously, the study of history makes one aware 'that what people *think* is true is often more important in its consequences than what is actually true'.[2]

A.V. Dicey had, as his main thesis, the close dependence of legislation upon the varying currents of public opinion in England during the nineteenth century, although his argument is weakened by his failure to define public opinion.[3] Peter Bartrip has recently argued in a similar vein that public opinion was 'of central importance in determining and justifying all public policy', defining public opinion as 'the sentiments expressed in Parliament or the pages of newspapers'.[4] Jennifer Davis, in arguing that it was the actions and reactions of the press, public and various government agencies involved in control which created the 1862 'crime wave' rather than any significant increase in criminal activity in the streets, believes that 'public' and 'public opinion' refer primarily, but not exclusively, to the middle and upper classes.[5] Gurr, Grabosky and Hula have observed that 'some groups' changing conceptions of order become influential enough to change the legal boundaries of disorderly behaviour'.[6] This follows a school of sociological thought[7] which argues that the explanation of crime can be found by studying the interests of the elites and institutions that selectively define and prosecute it. What is being argued, as we shall see in the following chapters of this study, is that essentially middle-class opinion can be mobilised to change the institutions of law and order but that such changes, apart from redefining crime, have little effect on the actual behaviour of deviant citizens. Gurr et al. defined their 'elite' which they regard as synonymous with 'ruling class' as the government, the

A PRACTICAL APPLICATION OF AN OLD PANTOMIME JOKE.

"*What's o'clock, you Scamp? Just struck One.*"

opposition party and 'those whose views they solicit and respond to including industrialists, trades union leaders, senior civil servants, many experts and intellectuals, and some of the media'. In the context of the nineteenth century when trades union leaders were not yet of the ruling elite, this motley collection of influential people would all fall within the category of upper and middle class. Such elites are not autonomous but subject to the constraints of their own values and social beliefs and the bureaucratic inertia of established police, judicial and penal systems, and that external pressure for change comes from the general public, special interest groups and 'intellectuals and experts who mould public opinion'.[8] As with Bartrip's 'sentiments expressed in parliament' one has to ask where did they come from? It is the argument of this study that these sentiments and the voice of the 'general public' and 'intellectuals and experts' were to be found in the newspapers of the day. It was in the letter columns and the editorials that the opinions of the ruling elite could be expressed, exchanged and changed. The only comparable institutions for the expression of ideas, in terms of the power base they influenced, were the clubs of Pall Mall and parliamentary select committees, neither of which gave open forum to the conventional middle-class opinions which are generally accepted to be the basis of influential 'public opinion'.

Peter Bartrip criticises Jenifer Davis for treating middle-class respectable opinion as if it was homogeneous. This is a trap into which one can easily be led by over-generalisation. At all times there is a divergence of view within the middle class. Such a divergence can be discerned in the mid-nineteenth century in Thomas Plint's *Crime in England* (1851) which denied the increase in juvenile crime claimed by such writers as Worsley, Beggs, Thomson, Rotch, Buchanan and Hill.[9] Within the heterogeneity of middle-class opinion there was normally a dominant argument (in our example that of those whom Plint criticised) and this is the one to which a power elite would refer. It is also that which the majority of newspapers would disseminate and support. *Reynolds' News*, as a socialist newspaper, was the only newspaper which would be likely to espouse an opinion contrary to that which was dominant for any great length of time. In general the influential newspapers would make an argument which their readership accepted or they would gradually bring their argument round to a more generally accepted consensus view. Thus middle-class views were not homogeneous but certain views were held by a majority of the middle classes, and these would be seen as the consensus view of the period.

Bartrip and Davis both agree that it was the mobilisation of public opinion which caused a change in the control structure of the 1860s.

They differ over what was the cause of the mobilisation. Davis argues that it was the garotting attack on Hugh Pilkington MP, whereas Bartrip believes that there is 'little justification for placing so much stress upon the garotting outbreak as a turning point' but that 'a far more important shock to respectable Victorian society was administered by the virtual termination of transportation in the 1850s'. Bartrip's damning conclusion that 'the answer to Davis's question as to whether the garotting panic deserves its obscure place in nineteenth-century historiography, is yes', is unnecessary and reveals a misunderstanding of the nature of moral panics. The inventory may have first been built on the initial deviance of the ticket-of-leave scares in the 1850s but it was the sensitisation produced by this initial inventory which created the environment for the 1862 garotting panic to occur. Cohen argued that one of the effects of the inventory is that the expectation is created that the form of deviance will recur while sensitisation has the effect that greater notice will be taken of signs of the deviance occurring. Bartrip states that he is unsure whether the outcry against the ticket-of-leave system was a groundswell of opinion, newspaper sensationalism, or parliamentary ignorance. All three are a product of the media for groundswells of opinion are created by constantly addressing the people (see Chapter 3) and much of the information and misinformation received by nineteenth-century members of parliament must have originated in the press. It is probable that the nineteenth-century backbenchers were less in tune with the opinion of the middle classes than those of today. They did not hold 'clinics' to hear their constituents' views as is the present practice, and so were largely dependent on the press for their information even on domestic matters. Davis sees the press as 'the instigator and mouthpiece of public opinion' and realises that if the media arouse public opinion sufficiently and create a strong enough panic then the authorities will take action. She acknowledged that 'it was the end of transportation and certainly not a rising crime rate which forced the public mind to think of convicts' but later correctly argues that, 'it was the garotting panic which focused criticism and aroused public opinion to an unprecedented pitch'.

Bartrip, discussing the outbreak of press criticism of the ticket-of leave system in 1855 notes that, 'a small number of serious crimes involving licences was magnified into a national crisis by newspapers which saw good copy in crime in general and ticket-of-leave scares in particular'. This was one of the many instances in which the middle classes were the unwitting pawns in the hands of a not-so-witless press in the process of manufacturing a crime wave.

In discussing the law and order panic over mugging in the media during the early 1980s a writer advises that 'these law and order tornadoes are recurrent. If there's a crime crisis, it's only unprecedented since the last one'. The description of the panic gives an impression of *déjà vu* to those with knowledge of the 1860s, for we are told that the debate in the House of Commons is the 'parliamentary climax to a month of clamour and rumour which has provided an open season for every crackpot theory and prejudice in the lexicon of crime and punishment'.[10] In his history of respectable fears, Geoffrey Pearson argues that the middle classes and respectable opinion are constantly rediscovering crime and violence in society and that what is interesting is the 'continual re-apperance of these ancient preoccupations as if they were "new" and unrivalled in their enormity'.[11] Pearson's review reveals the tunnel-vision of respectable opinion which constantly discovers the moral and physical deterioration of its youth, blaming it on permissiveness, excess material well-being, poor education and degenerate leisure activities, whilst constantly referring back to a mythical age when the young behaved as respectable opinion feels the young should behave. This meaningless rhetoric and misinformation is given an audience largely through the press. It would be interesting to discover how far the middle classes recognise it as meaningless rhetoric and the exposition of a myth and how far the subject matter of the myth, that is crime, causes genuine disquiet to members of the middle class. It would be hoped that as the myth was exposed over time the national psyche would change and learn to ignore it. The press has often exposed itself or other sections of itself as myth-making and yet the middle classes persist in supporting such sections of the press. In 1982 the *Daily Telegraph* noted that:

> Rape, of course, is suddenly everywhere in the newspapers and on television. The courts are thick with maligned women and brutal magistrates.
> This is not, of course, because rape is actually dramatically increasing. Sexual offences are at a ten year low.[12]

We have seen in Chapter 3 how many sections of the press in 1856 and 1862 acknowledged the press role in the manufacture of a panic. Yet the middle classes and respectable opinion are willing to buy newspapers which periodically create and perpetuate these myths. An explanation for this may be found in the fact that the subject of the myth is not in reality a major problem in middle-class life. Of course, twentieth-century attitudes and responses cannot be directly transferred to the Victorian age but it is interesting that in the 1980s the Conservative government, and hence a majority of the press, chose to make law and order an issue and yet in 1980, in England and Wales, there were 30 robberies per 100,000 population. In London, where the incidence of robbery was highest, there were 104 per 100,000. Given that the

LITTLE JONES (who of course is not a bit afraid of the Garotters), sotto voce. "*I wonder what the dooce that low-looking fellow means by always trying to get behind me.*"

majority of these incidents occur in areas of cities where the middle classes do not live and need not venture, the real threat to members of the respectable class is very low even in a time when the perceived threat is high. Consequently the middle-class reader can read a law and order debate in the press with the attitude of a detached, unaffected observer. The subject is not of primary concern to the reader who can view exaggeration and myth creation as another form of entertainment. There is an element of relaxation in reading of other people's problems and when the press rants against the 'fact' that it has become a middle-class problem the reader is aware that this is not a fact for he can walk, and has been walking, the streets he wishes to walk in near-perfect safety.

Gurr et al. conclude that since the mid-nineteenth century crime and public order in England in general and London in particular 'has rarely been more than a secondary concern for most of the elite or the public at large'. They believe one contributory factor was that the ruling elite believed they had the 'capacity to create a moral, industrious, prosperous – hence orderly – society' and that 'the conditions that bred the "criminal class" and crime were thought to be remediable'.[13] In the same volume David Pierce discerns a change in the attitude of the governing elite over the one hundred and fifty years to the present. He offers the hypothesis that in the first half of the nineteenth century the governing elite feared revolution and 'their potential allies, the rising commercial classes' felt threatened by common criminals as there was no efficient private or public protection from them. This led to an insistence that the institutions of law and order be improved. By the 1970s the 'more powerful and prosperous Londoners' live in 'safe' parts of the city; most material goods are insured and commercial establishments merely pass the cost of crime onto the customers. The main victims of crime who receive no compensation are the working classes and Pierce concludes, 'As long as they are the principal victims, there is little incentive for the Cabinet, the senior civil service, the academic experts and critics, or the press to improve the quality of public order'.[14]

One reason for crime and public order being only a secondary concern is that social behaviour in general took on a more civilised aspect throughout the nineteenth century. Whether this was a result of action by the middle classes or the state to create a moral, industrious and prosperous society is the subject of the next section.

II

During the nineteenth century there was a transformation of manners and behaviour. From a twentieth-century viewpoint it could be argued that life had become more civilised. This was evident in all areas of life. E.P. Thompson, for example, notes that towards the end of the eighteenth century the most characteristic complaint of the ruling classes was of the working classes' 'indiscipline ... their lack of economic dependency and their social insubordination'.[15] The beginning of the nineteenth century witnessed, argues Thompson, a period when many of the labour force were no longer under the social control of the manorial system but were not yet subject to the discipline of the factory. By the end of the century food riots and attacks on employers' property had been replaced by the more civilised well-organised demonstration and strike, and the street life had tended to go behind doors. The whole aspect of leisure became more civilised throughout the century with a decline in the brutal pastimes of cock- and badger-fighting, bull- and bear-baiting and the rough village ritual celebrations of Whitsuntide being replaced by association football, cycling, working men's clubs and the music hall.[16] Even the state became more civilised. Michael Ignatieff describes the transition in the penal system between 1750 and 1830 from an emphasis on punishment 'directed at the body' such as branding, whipping, the stocks and hanging 'being gradually replaced by incarceration "directed at the mind".'[17]

How did this transformation in manners and behaviour occur? The most obvious answer is that it resulted from social control, a process whereby the power elite in the country coerce the population to behave in an acceptable manner. Such an approach has many advocates[18] and can be argued quite plausibly. This social control, it is argued, was apparent in the three main areas of life of work, leisure and education, and in the role of the state.

Thompson has argued that early on in the nineteenth century the lower socio-economic group were disciplined by the work situation and he describes the degree of social control exercised by the masters in the form of the inculcation of such concepts as discipline, punctuality, regularity and routine.[19] The factory whistle was probably capable of exercising more social control than any of the institutions of state.

The second form of social control often alluded to is the imposition of middle-class, 'civilised', institutions on the working classes and the middle-class inspired destruction of working-class institutions. This argument usually focuses on education and leisure. At the turn of the century the traditional institutions of church and charity schools were discerned as failing in their aim of civilising the growing mass of urban poor. This led to the growth of Dissenting and Anglican schools in the 1830s, the more secular 'public' schools in the 1840s and culminated in the Education Act of 1870. Thus the middle-class values were transmitted to the lower orders via the education system. In the area of leisure it is accepted that there was an immense change amongst the working classes from activities 'defiled by animal-baiting, dancing and all manner of lewdness',[20] to more civilised pursuits. Bailey argues that this is a result of 'house training' of the working classes.[21] R.D. Storch in several articles has argued that the police were used in Northern England as instruments of social control under the influence of the Church and temperance lobbies on local policies to harry the working classes in their traditional activities of fair-going and loafing on street corners. F.M.L. Thompson has observed that:

> It is ironical that so many Victorians, whose ruling ideology is supposed to have been dedicated to the pursuit of the greatest happiness of the greatest number, should have spent so much time trying to throttle the happiness out of people'.[22]

Finally it is argued that the coercive powers of the state were a potent force in social control and the imposition of good manners and behaviour on the lower orders. The legislature, police, judiciary, penal system, military, poor law institutions and lunatic asylums were all used to keep the lower orders under control and goad them into respectability.

Such arguments are initially plausible but are perhaps distorted by a naive view of a simple two or three class society in which the ruling classes firstly can impose civilised behaviour on the lower classes and, secondly, have a model of civilised behaviour to impose. It can be argued that the accepted instruments of social control did not wholly fulfil their function and that the transformation in manners and behaviour was a result, not of social control, but of a process of socialisation whereby people develop and acquire the cultural values of society, rather than have them imposed upon them. Such a viewpoint would argue that leisure was not transformed by the introduction of public parks, libraries, reading rooms and working men's clubs under the auspices of temperance societies and Church, but as a result of the two related trends of the commercialism of leisure with the growth of an entertainments industry and the rise of organised sport. Hence the public house declined in relative popularity in the 1890s not under temperance pressure but as it was eclipsed by the popularity of the music hall. The growth of organised sport after 1870 reveals a process of the working classes taking over middle-class institutions and adapting them to their needs. Football is the classic example of this process, starting as

PUNCH, OR THE LONDON CHARIVARI.—NOVEMBER 29, 1862.

THE GAROTTER'S FRIEND.

"LET GO, BILL, CAN'T YER—IT'S OUR KIND NON-INTERFERING FRIEND, SIR GEORGE GREY!!!"

a public school and university game and by the 1880s becoming a working-class spectator sport with all the aspects of channelled aggression which it has today. Pitch invasions, attacks on referees and players, and fighting between rival fans were commonplace and led Ernest Ensor to conclude, in 1898, that 'the old English feeling for "sport" and "fair play" has receded to thinly-populated or remote districts where athletes cannot be exploited for money'.[23]

In education, 'socialisers', as opposed to 'social controllers', believe that the schools failed in their aims of spreading moralistic teachings throughout the lower orders who merely used such institutions to acquire the skills of literacy and numeracy and ignored the attempts to transmit middle-class morality. This seems to be an overstatement of the case, for the Education Act of 1870 may not have succeeded in its aims of moral education but it did ensure that the majority of those of school age were attending an institution which in itself constituted a form of social control. It may, however, be argued that this was a result of socialisation, as the respectable working classes chose to have their children educated, and that the state was performing an enabling rather than a coercive role.

The inadequacy of the coercive power of the state to exercise social control is clearly demonstrated by the Security from Violence Act of 1863 which re-introduced flogging for the crime of robbery with violence. It demonstrated the failure of the state to prevent crime and the inadequacy of the moral attitude of the ruling elite to provide a model to which the lower orders could aspire if they wished to be civilised. In 1862, the panic year which provoked the legislation, street violence accounted for 8.9 per cent of those committed for trial at Quarter Sessions or Assizes in London, 15.5 per cent in Liverpool and 3.7 per cent in Manchester. The percentage was exceeded twenty-one times in the twenty-five years following the legislation in London, eleven times up to 1892 in Liverpool and in every year during this period in Manchester. Such statistics indicate a failure of the state legislature to exercise any substantial degree of control. The state's message was clearly not being communicated adequately by means of the birch.

That the 'civilised' behaviour of the ruling elite was hardly an adequate model is also illustrated by the Security from Violence Act. It was enacted within the context of a belief that beating constituted perfectly civilised behaviour and that to spare the rod was to spoil the child. Pearson has demonstrated that the moral landscape of the 1860s included flogging as acceptable behaviour.[24] It was an everyday occurrence in the centres of educational excellence and was used widely in the army and navy to maintain morale and discipline. It was also the accepted method of controlling the empire. As a result of the Whipping Act of 1865 in India 75,000 were flogged in 1878 alone, a figure which had only crept down to 64,078 by 1897. Governor Eyre's action in putting down the Morant Bay rising in Jamaica in 1865 by using troops to massacre 600, executing many hundreds and by wide-spread flogging included the lashing of women on bare buttocks with piano wire caused an initial controversy, but soon resulted in Parliament's endorsement of Eyre's action and *The Times*'s condemnation of his critics.[25]

It would appear that social control was not the mechanism by which the remarkable transformation of manners occurred. Several factors which would have encouraged the socialisation of a more civilised society may be proffered. It seems evident that the discipline of the work situation was paramount, if not in active social control, in at least encouraging socialisation by offering the means of betterment. Housing and civic improvements and the various public health measures provided a more 'civilised' environment. Similarly, economic growth in general made possible an improvement in living standards so that material betterment provided a basis for an improvement in social behaviour. A larger and more professional police force, rather than imposing social control, gave people confidence to act in a respectable way. To create an environment in which people can act in a respectable way seems to be essential. Harold Perkin[26] sees emulation as a key explanatory factor although his emulation is that of the working classes of the middle classes and the middle classes of the ruling classes. This cannot be entirely the case for, as we have seen, certain aspects of middle-class behaviour were not civilised in the twentieth-century sense. However, socialisation does occur with the emulation of one section of individuals in the society by others. Hence one respectable working-class family could set the tone and become the standard for the rest of the street. One liberal reformer could prick the conscience and cause an alteration of behaviour in a whole section of middle-class society.

Thus, throughout the century, behaviour in general became more civilised as a result of socialisation rather than social control and the class which most keenly associated itself with this growth of respectability and benefited most from it were those in the middle. The remainder of this chapter describes how the middle classes reacted to the reported outbreaks of violence in London, Liverpool and Manchester which were in sharp contrast to the otherwise discernible trend of increasingly civilised behaviour of society in general.

TO GAROTTERS.—"CAVE TOMKINS."

TOMKINS (*loq.*). "*Let 'em try it on again, that's all.*"

III

A man and his wife were jostled and attacked with violence by some roughs. 'My hat was deliberately knocked off and trodden upon'. The assailants fled, 'but not before one of them had felt the weight of my stick'. The fact that such an outrage can be perpetrated, with probable impunity, in a broad and much frequented thorough-fare, will I trust, be accepted by you, Sir, as a fair reason for troubling you with this letter.

Letter from 'XYZ', *The Times*, 26 June 1876

All societies are beset with problems which invariably are ever-present but are only identified as problems when the established institutions of the society, (the government, the judiciary, law enforcement agencies, the press) have occasion to focus their attention on them. We, in the twentieth century, are in the privileged position to be one hundred years of problem-solving ahead of our Victorian forebears and are in a time in which many of the problems which faced Victorian society are no longer regarded as problems as their solutions are known. The probability of gas explosions demolishing the whole of London or of suffocation when travelling in open railway trains at speeds in excess of ten miles per hour are examples. In the nineteenth century society was still facing problems of a basic nature such as the whole gamut of public health, medical health, transport, cyclical unemployment, a new social structure, the growth of cities, etc. Not only are twentieth-century society's problems more sophisticated and more narrowly defined but this society also possesses a more sophisticated machinery for problem solving. This is not to suggest that any society is faced with a set store of problems which may be gradually eroded until Utopia is reached. Each society throws up new problems and re-defines old ones. The Victorians, for example, were not faced with the threat of a nuclear holocaust or oil pollution. There are some phenomena which exist both in Victorian society and in present-day society which the twentieth century has the luxury of defining as problems but which the Victorians were forced to accept as an acceptable part of everyday life. Tooth decay is such an example. Whereas present-day society can afford the luxury of identifying dental caries as a problem and hotly debate whether the water system should be fluoridated, the Victorians were still at the stage of solving the problem of how to build a water system. The pain of a Victorian tooth-ache was nonetheless just as real as it is today. The 'rough' – the hooligan element – was probably as prevalent in Victorian society as he is today but (except in the specific cases cited in the previous sections) was not identified as a problem and was accepted as a natural facet of the social structure to such an extent that he did not really get a mention until the last quarter of the century.

A letter from 'M' written to *The Times* in November 1881, gives a feeling of the encounter between the gentle and the rough in what is a minor incident. A man and his wife were riding their double tricycle along the King's Road, Chelsea, when a rough flung himself and lay down in their path, 'nearly flinging both of us from our seats'. The rough jumped up laughing and the man threatened to put him into custody. The rough then

> ... rushed at me, swearing horribly and struck at my face three times; one blow just touched my cheek, and at the same moment I gave him a return on the forehead which knocked him down. He was instantly surrounded by his fellows and in another moment was rushing away. No one raised a hand or spoke a word in my defence and nothing but the most diabolical mischief could have induced the man to act this way.[27]

This incident illustrates not only the frustration and inadequacy of the middle-class victim but also the motivation which triggers the ruffian's action, for as Henry Mayhew observed, 'if the Metropolitan "roughs" belong to the dangerous classes, they form a large part of the humorous, devil-may-care section of society also'.[28] This devil-may-care attitude comes across very strongly in most reports of incidents and it was this difference in attitude and values that the middle classes recognised and feared. The rough did not play by the rules. He did not, for example, recognise the authority of the police. In 1887 a rough forced his way into a house at Essex Villas, Kensington, and abusively demanded a tip. 'He only left when the Policeman appeared in the street, and then he only strolled away, for, as he stated, he did not care for all the police in London'.[29]

Ruffianism was undoubtedly a permanent feature of big city life. *The Times* placed it in perspective by arguing that if the figures were carefully examined it would be shown that the dangers from crimes of violence were far less than the dangers from 'vehicles driven along our streets with reckless speed and contempt for the lives and limbs of those on foot'.[30] The problem for the middle classes was not so much the physical violence, however, as the intellectual or emotional violence – the blow to the pride. George Orwell, writing in 1937, captures this with his observation that anyone over thirty could remember the time when well-dressed people could not walk in certain quarters of the big towns without being hooted at. 'The London gutterboy everywhere, with his loud voice and lack of intellectual scruples, could make life a misery for people who considered it beneath their dignity to answer back'.[31]

A HINT
TO PARTIES WHO RESIDE IN A GAROTTING NEIGHBOURHOOD.

The roughs were not defined as a problem by the middle classes or their press. Like tooth-ache they were one of the less pleasurable aspects of their world but few thought that they could be done away with. The folk devils produced by the moral panics engendered by the press were defined as problems and produced a middle-class reaction. Much of this reaction involved criticism of the police, the penal system and the legislature which is covered in the following chapters, but the panics also produced a movement towards self-protection.

IV

If a few resolute pedestrians, whose business keeps them out late at night, are determined to maintain at all hazards, their right of walking the streets at any hour, and in the vindication of this right should succeed in inflicting summary punishment on the savage pirates that now infest our thoroughfares, the lesson may be a salutary one and in any case no great harm will be done. But the desire to legalise this species of reprisals, by importing a vindictive spirit into the law, is an evil far greater and far more to be dreaded.

Daily News, 4 December 1862

Much of the following account will strike the reader as humorous. It is difficult to comprehend for a reader who lives in a society where public protection is almost wholly designated to a largely trusted and technically efficient police force, where streets are well lit and where the majority of the public finds the carrying of weapons an alien act and no longer reveres the character-building attributes of fist-fighting. In Victorian times the speedy arrival of the police could not be counted upon. There were no telephones, no two-way radios, no 120 m.p.h. patrol cars with flashing lights and sirens. There was, with luck, a police constable somewhere in the area with a rattle to call his colleagues and his legs to get him there. Such points are obvious, but it is too easy for the modern reader to forget the quantity and quality of technological innovation which has so altered every facet of our lives which allows us to find humorous a situation which, for the Victorian, was deadly serious. It is in fact the lack of technological sophistication – the quaintness of it all – that seems to give the situations humour, although the Victorians themselves managed to laugh at their own over-reaction to the panics and their fantasising about the possible treatment of the perpetrators of street violence.

Punch was among the first periodicals to urge the public to protect themselves. It argued for an increase in the police and a greater severity of the application of the law 'but the public meanwhile must, according to their own disposition, take precautions to secure safety for life and property'.[32] *Punch* recommended the carrying of a well-weighted walking-stick and the 'new and approved knuckle-duster'. In the same year the *Illustrated Times* noted the general lack of ability of the populace to defend itself since the end of fencing and prize-fighting. It noted the over-reliance on the police and reminded its readers that, 'he who carries a sense of personal readiness and fitness to meet danger about with him, is not only a better man physically – he is a better man morally – than his less developed and trained neighbour'. The writer of the article believed that a group of such peopled armed with life-preservers (i.e. coshes) 'would make short work of half an army of the sweepings of the jails'.[33] Following the death of Richard Morgan, *The Porcupine* also called the attention of the populace to their own declining physical and moral standards. *The Porcupine* allowed itself to fantasise and gave the following account of the sort of reaction they expected:

> We recollect an instance in point. One night a young man, with his sweetheart on his arm, was walking quietly up Church Street, when three half-drunken roughs, who were arm-in-arm, and who had already hustled several passengers off the pathway, came along, and endeavoured to push him and the lady into the gutter. The young fellow at once disengaged from his companion and placed her in a doorway for safety. There being no policeman near to appeal to, he quietly turned back his cuffs, buttoned his coat, and selecting the biggest of the three youths for attack, knocked him down. The other bullies swore some muderous oaths, and rushed upon him with the view of getting him down, and of course kicking him; but he dexterously evaded their attack, and felled them both to the ground in succession. He then drew down his cuffs, unbuttoned his coat, gave his arm again to the young lady, and passed on up the street as though nothing had happened.'[34]

This was the model to which all middle-class persons aspired. As many did not possess the physical prowess to support such calm action and under the moral pressure from the press many armed themselves. 'By this time the cutlers and walking-stick makers must have pretty well cleared out their stock of dagger-knives, life-preservers and loaded bludgeons'.[35] The *Daily News* warned in December 1862 that if the garotting continued then the populace would form vigilante committees which would take the law into their own hands and hang ruffians from lamp-posts. 'Already the dealers in knives, and leaded sticks and revolvers are driving a brisk trade'. T. Lloyd-Baker, looking back on the panic of 1867, wrote that, 'there was more danger of an honest man being shot or stabbed by timorous gentlemen than of his being garotted by a rough'.[36]

The panic led to a rise in the number of absurd inventions under the name of anti-garotte stocks or collars. The Metropolitan Police Historical Museum, which is not open to the public, contains an example of a spiked collar which was designed to be worn by a gentleman underneath a cravat to prevent the garotter attacking the throat. In 1862 the *Daily News* summarised the available weaponry thus:

> No exaggeration that the most fanciful pantomime author can indulge in will caricature the armed condition of our citizens. Revolvers and bowie-knives are simple weapons compared to the arms which some self-defenders carry. Elaborate knuckle-dusters have been made to order, and containing one sharp stiletto protruding from the side. Bludgeons that shoot out bayonets, and sticks that contain daggers and swords are now sold more openly in the city streets than oranges and chestnuts. One belt at least has been seen the buckle of which is loaded like a pistol, and which, when a string is pulled under the coat of the wearer, will shoot anyone in front in the stomach. Life-preservers and thick sticks are more common than tooth-picks, and spiked collars are worn very generally with patriotic pleasure.[37]

The *Daily News* had prefaced this editorial with the remark that, 'the garotte panic has now probably reached its height, is a little on the decline, and is furnishing food for farce writers and arrangers of pantomime'. *Punch* was quick to laugh at people's ideas for self-protection although *Punch* itself was the first to publicise and advocate the use of the anti-garotte collar.[38] For those who were not prepared to arm themselves or wear armour, advice poured in to the letter columns of the press and was given in the literature, much of it seemingly based on the theory that Victorian Britain comprised a race of bionic super-heroes; and much was down-to-earth but conflicting.

Joseph Kingsmill, the Chaplain of Pentonville Prison, advised that 'the best way to foil an attack is to press down the chin to the chest ... allow the lungs full play, and then make good use of them, men and women alike screaming lustily. At a good shout the robbers will run.'[39] However, H.W. Holland, writing in *Good Words*, advised to the contrary,

> A solitary individual in the hands of garotters has only one chance, and that is to be quiet. Resistance only brings severer physical punishment to the helpless victim, who, being in their hands, is entirely at their mercy.[40]

Such a tame (perhaps sane) suggestion may have passed in 1866 but in

THE SONG OF THE GAROTTER.

H, meet me by moon-
light alone,
And then I will give
you the hug,
With my arm round
your neck tightly
thrown,
I'm as up to the work
as a Thug.
Behind you I softly
will creep,
And, taking you quite
unawares,
On my prey like a
tiger I'll leap;
If I happen to choke
you, who cares?

I'm out with a ticket
of leave,
Which by gulling the
chaplain I got,
And I'm free to
maim, murder and
thieve,
For a cove he must
live, must he
not?

So meet me by moonlight alone,
Kind stranger, I beg and entreat,
And I'll make all your money my own,
And leave you half dead in the street.

the 1850s such utterances condoning inaction were tantamount to blasphemy. 'Self Defence' offered the following 'more scientific defence' for the man in the street:

> The counter movement to which I allude, consists in throwing back your right leg and entwining it tightly round the leg of your foe; then by throwing the entire weight of your body upon him, no effort of his can save him from going down and you uppermost. The charm once broken, the game is your own; so if you feel sufficient confidence in yourself, you can give the scoundrel 'a one, two for his nob' by way of refresher. This is the only defence against sudden attack to be relied upon.[41]

J.C. Gregeory, who described himself as a 'tolerably good wrestler' asked 'Self Defence', 'How does he suppose his grandmother could manage to twist her right leg round that of her assailant?' and agreed with Kingsmill that for the non-athletic to keep the chin down and kick the assailant's shins was the best method. However, for the 'active man with good nerve' Gregory suggested the use of the 'flying mare':

> Seize the arm placed round your neck with both hands, pull it forward, then quickly bend your face down towards your toes, and you will be astonished with what ease you throw your adversary over your head.[42]

James Greenwood's garotter friend counselled that prevention was better than cure. He advised buttoning up the coat, wearing a soft scarf around the neck and carrying a short stick attached to the wrist with a leather strap. He also noted that it was best to walk down the middle of the road and 'never on the path where the shadow of a wall or hedge may conceal a lurker'.[43]

It was only the metropolitan garotting panics and the aftermath of Trafalgar Square in 1886 which truly reached the level of panic and inculcated real individual fears in the middle classes. Following the Trafalgar Square riot in 1886 the reports of the events on the Monday put people's nerves to the test and the middle classes and tradesmen were prepared to listen to any rumour if it was horrific enough. On the Tuesday the police over-compensated and put on a show of strength with the reserves on duty and the Guards on the alert. This, in itself, heightened the tension among the middle classes. On the Wednesday, 'London was thrown into a state of utter panic owing to the alarming rumours'. It was said that 10,000 were marching from Deptford. Although there was no truth in the rumour.

> London from one end to the other experienced another sharp spasm of

alarm with respect to rioters, and from the heart of the City to the far off suburbs preparations were made to meet the bands of ruffians stated to be on the march.[44]

Even the police seemed to mistrust themselves in, what the *Daily News* called, this 'ridiculous scare',[45] and advised shopkeepers to put up their shutters. The *Daily News* went on to explain,

> The panic which seized on a great part of the metropolis in the afternoon had no real foundation ... but the present generation has never experienced such a sense of insecurity of distrust in the arrangements for keeping order in the streets, as has spread over the metropolis since the miserable events of Monday afternoon.

This was the significance of the Trafalgar Square riot of 1886. For a time the roughs had ruled the West End and the police had failed to control them. They had temporarily ruled, not in any political sense but in the real and frightening way that a gang of hooligans rule in the place where they happen to be on those odd occasions when the police fail to control them. The very presence of the roughs, incongruous to West End life, was enough to frighten the middle classes.

V

Cohen's model showed an inventory and sensitisation, greatly aided by the press, leading to an over-estimation of the deviance which leads on to an escalation of the control culture. In section I of this chapter it has been argued that the middle classes rarely viewed crime as more than a secondary concern; one reason for this was the growing civilisation of the lower orders described in section II. The following chapters deal with the escalation in the control culture. As has been argued in section II, such social control was not necessarily effective but it was demanded. Perhaps it was fitting that the myth of the statistics and the press-manufactured folk devils should be countered with the myth of social control. Although of secondary importance to the middle classes, crime was a problem and at such times as the press brought it to their attention they used the press to prevail upon the institutions of social control, paid for by their rates and taxes, to do their duty – and escalate control. The following chapters trace the effects of these demands on the police, the legislature and the justices.

Notes

1. R. Lane, 'Urbanisation and criminal violence in the nineteenth-century: Massachussetts as a test case', in H. Davis Graham and T. Gurr (eds), *The History of Violence in America* (1969), 482.
2. B. Norling, *Timeless Problems in History* (1970), 1.
3. A.V. Dicey, *Lectures on Relations between Law and Public Opinion in England during the Nineteenth-Century* (1905), 1.
4. P.W. Bartrip, 'Public opinion and law enforcement: The Ticket-of-Leave scares in mid-Victorian Britain', in V. Bailey (ed.), *Policing and Punishment in Nineteenth-Century Britain* (1982).
5. J. Davis, 'The London Garotting Panic of 1862: A Moral Panic and the Creation of a Criminal Class in mid-Victorian Britain', in V.A.C. Gatrell, B. Lenman and G. Parker, eds., *Crime and the Law: The Social History of Crime in Western Europe since 1500* (1980).
6. T.R. Gurr, P.N. Grabosky and R.C. Hula, *The Politics of Crime and Conflict: A Comparative History of Four Cities* (1977), 6.
7. For example, R. Quinney, *The Social Reality of Crime* (1970); *Critique of Legal Order* (1973); A. Turk, *Criminality and Legal Order* (1969).
8. Gurr et al., op.cit.
9. H. Worsley, *Juvenile Depravity* (1849); T. Beggs, *An Inquiry into the Extent and Causes of Juvenile Depravity* (1849); A. Thomson, *Social Evils: Their Causes and Their Cure* (1852); B. Rotch, *Suggestions for the Prevention of Juvenile Depravity* (1846); W. Buchanan, *Remarks on the Causes and State of Juvenile Crime in the Metropolis* (1846); M. Hill, *Juvenile Delinquency* (1853).
10. 'A hit and myth debate', *New Society*, 25 March 1982.
11. G. Pearson, *Hooligan: A History of Respectable Fears* (1983), 213.
12. *Daily Telegraph*, 22 January 1982.
13. Gurr et al., op.cit., 680.
14. Ibid., 207.
15. E.P. Thompson, 'Patrician Society, Plebian Culture', *Journal of Social History* (1974), Vol. 7, 382–405.
16. For accounts of changes in leisure activity see, J. Walvin, *Leisure and Society, 1830–1950*, (1978): P. Bailey, *Leisure and Class in Victorian England: Rational Recreation and the Contest for Control, 1830–85* (1978); T. Mason, *Association Football and English Society* 1863–1915, (1980); H. Perkin, 'The "social tone" of the Victorian seaside resorts', in *The Structured Crowd* (1981); B. Harrison, *Drink and the Victorians* (1971).
17. M. Ignatieff, *A Just Measure of Pain: The Penitentiary in the Industrial Revolution 1750–1850*, (1978).
18. See, for example, A.P. Donajgrodzki (ed.), *Social Control in Nineteenth-Century Britain* (1977); Bailey, op.cit.; P. McCann (ed.), *Popular Education and Socialisation in Nineteenth-Century Britain* (1977).
19. E.P. Thompson, 'Time, Work Discipline and Industrial Capitalism', *Past and Present*, 38, (1967), 56–97.

20. E.P. Thompson, op.cit., (1974).
21. Bailey, op.cit., 174.
22. F.M.L. Thompson, 'Social Control in Victorian Britain', *Economic History Review*, 2nd series, XXXIV, 2 May (1981).
23. E. Ensor, 'The Football Madness', *Contemporary Review*, 74, November (1898) 751–60.
24. Pearson, op.cit., 150–153.
25. See B. Semmel, *The Governor Eyre Controversy* (1962).
26. H. Perkin, *Origins of Modern English Society, 1780–1880*, (1951).
27. Letter from 'M' *The Times*, 21 November 1881.
28. H. Mayhew, *London Characters* (1881), 345.
29. Letter from 'M.B.H.', *The Times*, 21 October 1887.
30. *The Times*, 5 January 1884.
31. G. Orwell, *The Road to Wigan Pier*, (1937).
32. *Punch*, 19 November 1856.
33. *Illustrated Times*, 6 December 1856.
34. *The Porcupine*, 19 December 1874.
35. *Illustrated Times*, 24 January 1863.
36. T.B. Lloyd-Baker, *War with Crime* (1889), 20.
37. *Daily News*, 19 December 1862.
38. *Punch*, 27 September 1856.
39. Letter from J. Kingsmill, *The Times*, 3 January 1857.
40. H.W. Holland, 'The Art of Self-Protection against Thieves and Robbers', *Good Words*, December 1866, 851.
41. Letter from 'Self Defence', *The Times*, 6 January 1857.
42. Letter from J.C. Gregory, *The Times*, 9 January 1857.
43. J. Greenwood, *The Policeman's Lantern: Strange Stories of London Life*, (1888).
44. *Reynolds' Weekly Newspaper* 14 February 1886.
45. *Daily News*, 11 February 1886.

6. The Effect of the Panics on the Police – their Image and Response

This is, in the horrible slang of the times a 'sensation' year in town, and among the excitements provided for our foreign and provincial visitors, is garotting at night in the principal thoroughfares, which the police authorities, by way of a picturesque revival of the good old times, are kind enough to authorise at least by the non-interference by the reputed guardians of the public safety.

Daily News, 18 July 1862

I

An obvious modern reaction to any outbreak of crime is to criticise police inaction or police inefficiency. Such a reaction is often based on ignorance of the real problems which the police face, or of the action which, in fact, the police are taking but which they cannot publicise. In modern society the protection of the citizen is a role wholly delegated to the police. People fear and hate violent criminals who terrorise them and are interested only in the use of force by the police as a solution to the problem.

In the early nineteenth century this was not exactly so. It was common for an armed man-servant to sleep where the household silver was kept, it was not unusual for several men to be killed in affrays between poaching gangs and armed bodies of gamekeepers and it was unremarkable for a gentleman to carry a sword for his own protection. Much of the responsibility for the safeguarding of person and property still rested with the individual citizen. It was during the nineteenth century, and partly as a result of the moral panics, that the emphasis on self-protection shifted towards police protection.

A second change is indicated by Roger Lane's model to account for the fact that in Boston, Massachusetts, during the nineteenth century as a whole the serious crime rate was falling whilst the total crime rate was rising.[1] The model is that of a fall in the real crime rate allowing officially accepted standards of conduct to rise. As these standards rise, the machinery of justice is extended and refined, thus resulting in an increase in the total number of cases whilst there is a decrease in their relative severity.

Throughout the century the duties, powers and authority of the police were extended and refined and they were increasingly used, not to control the dangerous classes and prevent the overthrow of civilised society, but to harry the working classes and prevent nuisances.[2] The panics served to remind a public of the primary object of the employment of the police (that is the suppression of serious crime) at a time when the public began to accept that the police were automatically performing this duty and was more concerned with developing secondary objects for police activity. In addition to the prevention of crime, the police were responsible for the smooth flow of traffic, collecting the votes for the Poor Law guardians and in 1851, they delivered and collected the census papers. From 1845 they assisted the Inland Revenue in checking that duties were paid on stage coaches and in 1851 were made responsible for the inspection and supervision of Common Lodging Houses. In 1853 the police were charged with enforcing the Smoke Abatement Act. They were also responsible for missing persons, lost property, transporting drunks to the station house (normally in a hand cart) and escorting prisoners to and from court and prison. The police in the metropolis proved to be good value and gradually won the respect of the upper and middle classes who paid the police rate. By 1852 the *Edinburgh Review*[3] noted that citizens now regarded it as a matter of course 'that they sleep and awake in safety in the midst of hordes of starving plunderers'. In 1870 the *Quarterly Review*[4] referred to the Metropolitan Police as 'a sober, vigilant and intelligent body of men . . . the like of which, perhaps, does not exist in any country'. The police during the nineteenth century were mainly recruited amongst out-of-work tradesmen and discharged soldiers. They were poorly paid (having to supplement their wages by knocking people up and asking for Christmas boxes) and rigorously disciplined.

The tasks of the police were many and varied but it was soon realised that, although perhaps not always helpful to the working classes, they were not a body being used as an overtly repressive force by a tyrannical government. The tasks of a man on patrol were listed by the *Quarterly Review* in 1870 as possessing a thorough knowledge of the streets and the inhabitants of the houses on the beat; checking that door fastenings were secure; reporting uncovered coal holes and trap doors; observing suspicious loiterers and paying particular attention to public houses and beer-shops although 'he is not to enter except in the immediate execution of his duty'. He also had to report all nuisances (including smoking chimneys, street noises and stray dogs) and look after beggars, tramps, lost children, accident cases and disorderly persons obstructing highways or causing a breach of the peace. He had to watch pillar boxes and report if street lamps were not properly lighted. He was supposed to report dangerous houses or structures and help extinguish fires before the arrival of the fire brigade, and take care of any exposed property. He was expected to prevent soliciting by prostitutes and take appropriate action to prevent offences against morality generally including the seizure of obscene prints and publications. On all these matters the police had special instructions which had to be memorised.

It was during the period of the panics that the public came to perceive the police as the institution to supply the force necessary to protect them against the mob and against criminals. Prior to the nineteenth century urban disorder was not necessarily perceived as subversive of the social order but Storch has noted in another article, that by the 1830s and 1840s the dred of the 'dangerous classes' could be transformed into near hysteria at times of great social and political tension.[5] The 'crime-wave' of the 1860s – 'perhaps more apparent than real' – led to a redefinition of the dangerous classes by the public and 'sanctioned a more precise sorting out of target groups who might be made the objects of an extensive scope of police control'.[6] The main new target group was the ticket-of-leave men, for one of the results of the panics was to show that the public viewed the primary role of the police as preventing crime rather than revolution. They were required to protect the individual and not the social structure.

It was during this period from the 1840s to the 1870s that the public began wholly to delegate the role of protection to the police and so it was during this period that the public began to question police efficiency. Such criticism took two distinct forms. One form questioned the efficiency of the force as a force – its organisation, its leadership, its philosophy regarding the treatment of criminals. The second took the form of criticism of the individual policemen that made up the force – their courage, their ability, their enthusiasm for the job. Both forms of criticism were a result of two inter-related strands. One was the frustration or feeling of impotence engendered by the garotting scares. The other was the growing realisation of the increasing importance of the role of the police in the maintenance of law and order, and the protection of the individual. The feeling of impotence led the individual to realise that he could not fight the criminal alone and must place greater reliance on the police to execute the task on his behalf. The individual was therefore entitled to criticise the police if he felt they were not performing the task. 'In these days we have abdicated our individual right to protect our property and persons to Judges and Police constables', wrote a correspondent to *The Times* in 1885, so that anyone suffering robbery or violence, especially from a criminal whom the courts have freed 'has a distinct grievance against those who administer justice for non-fulfilment of an implied contract'.[7] It was clearly understood that the function of the police constable was to harass the criminal classes. 'If he exhibits a kind of unreasoning, watchdog antagonism towards the criminal classes', wrote James Greenwood in 1869, it was because he was paid to act against them 'whenever he finds plausible excuse for doing so' and that 'so long as the constable remains a well-regulated machine and fulfils his functions without jarring or unnecessary noise, we will ask no more'.[8]

The police were essentially an organisation paid for by and employed to serve the middle classes. Emsley believes that 'in general policemen appear to have been more civil to members of the middle class than to members of the working class' as a result of the stereotypical image of the criminal as working class.[9] 'The 'public' (meaning the middle and upper classes) ... held their "bobby" in patronising "affection and esteem" which he repaid with due respectfulness', wrote Roberts in his description of Salford slum life in the first quarter of the twentieth century, 'but these sentiments were never shared by the undermass, nor, in fact, by the working class generally'.[10] The police in Northern England were established as a result of a 'new consensus among the propertied classes', according to Storch, 'that it was necessary to create a professional, bureaucratically organised lever of urban discipline' so that it could be permanently introduced 'into the heart of working-class communities'.[11] It was always police policy to observe working-class areas in order to protect middle-class residential areas. Hence Charles Rowans's oft-quoted axiom that 'We look upon it that we are guarding St James's and other places while we are watching St Giles and bad places in general'.[12]

The middle classes undoubtedly perceived the police as their public servants, with the emphasis on servant. Charles Dickens the Younger asked the Metropolitan Police department whether the police on night duty were available for calling private individuals in time for early trains. The answer that they 'are taught that they are bound to render this or any other service in their power' and that failure to do so is 'considered a breach of duty, and dealt with accordingly'[13] fairly illustrates the point.

The police were often despised by the working classes. The process by which the police provoked the working classes in the streets by enforcing a 'move-on system' as standard police policy and by repressing and interferring with their traditional leisure activities, e.g. drinking, gambling and brutal sports has been well described by Storch in his three articles.

On one point the middle and working classes were agreed. It was a common belief and joke that police constables spent too much time in the servants' quarters of houses when they should have been on their beats. It was inevitably *Punch* which took up the theme on behalf of the middle classes, referring to the police as 'those invisible blue-bottles that haunt our larders a great deal more than our streets'.[14] 'It having become proverbial that the Police are only to be found when they are not wanted, and there being no case on record of their having ever yet come up in time to prevent a garotte robbery', wrote the directors in the imaginary prospectus of the 'Anti-Garotte Assurance Company' they had decided that, 'whilst the "force" has a weakness for cooks and sausage suppers',[15] it was necessary to adopt other measures to ensure the protection of the public. Steedman has argued that the police were the obvious butt of humorists as they represented members of the working classes who had 'tried to become among those who govern and manage'.[16]

The main complaint levelled at the police during the panics was that they were never there when required. The inference was that they were not on their beats (as shown above) or that they preferred to keep to the safer parts of their beat where trouble was least likely to be encountered. The charge was more common in the 1856 panic than in later episodes. *The Times* letter columns bristled with cries of 'there were no police'[17] 'where are the police when most wanted, and for what purpose do we pay police rates?';[18] 'It is so well known that policemen are never where they ought to be';[19] 'at the time of the occurrence there was no policeman in sight',[20] and 'it is a rarity to see a policeman'.[21] However, *The Times* gave little editorial support to the blame-the-police lobby, preferring to save their venom for a penal system which freed prisoners on ticket-of-leave. The editor was of the opinion that 'at this moment in London the police could, if authorised, make a clean sweep of well-nigh all the garotters, burglars and violent vagabonds'.[22] This was a view echoed in 1870 by the *Quarterly Review* which argued that 'it is not the police who are really in fault, so much as that tenderness for scoundrelism of all kinds that has become one of the pervading follies of our time'. In 1862 the letter columns found the police blameless, although the editors were less charitable. The *Daily News* wrote of 'those stiff and full-fed figures in blue' and observed 'there are plenty of them wherever they are not wanted'.[23] *The Times* changed its tack in mid panic. Before the November sessions it was of the opinion that 'such outrages as those we have recently had to report are in the first degree disgraceful to the police'[24] and that 'the police are not blameless in the matter'[25] but this was never a full-blooded attack and after the Sessions it had decided that 'the police are doing a good deal, and deserve much credit'.[26]

These attacks on the police are symptomatic of the panic situation. The public had grown to believe that the police were their sole protectors. When this protection was found not to be one hundred per cent perfect the first natural disposition was to attack the police. After reflection it was apparent that the police were trying to do a difficult job to the best of their ability although the demands placed upon them were too many. It occurred to only a few that 'no police, however numerous, can always be watching every street in a place like London'[27] or that even the uneducated criminal classes had the common sense not to commit a crime when there was a policeman in close proximity. The *Illustrated Times* also supported the police and disputed that they were not present on their beats in large enough numbers. A walk with a police inspector found 'ghostly-looking constables' who 'loom suddenly from the dark shadows of courts and over-hanging gateways' and proved that 'the popular opinion must soon be classed with many other exploded fallacies'.[28]

The organisation and administration of the police was criticised but not during the periods of panic. As early as 1843 'L' wrote that it was strange that London should have so many robbers, 'boasting as it does, of possessing such a well-organised body of police'.[29] In 1868 a delegation was received by Bruce, the Home Secretary, of delegates from all the districts of London led by three members of parliament in order to make statements 'as to the increase of robberies with violence in the streets of London and reflecting upon the alleged inefficiency of the police'. The delegates were addressed by a Professor Marks who remarked that the metropolis was 'almost entirely dependent upon the police force' for its protection. Despite the increase in police numbers, crime was on the increase and Professor Marks attributed this 'to the inefficiency of the force, an inefficiency attributed to its organisation'.[30] Such an attack was aimed at Sir Richard Mayne who was entering his fortieth year as metropolitan commissioner. Mayne always had the support of the Queen and after his death in 1869 her private secretary wrote to the Home Secretary of her grief and that 'notwithstanding the attacks lately made upon him, Her Majesty believes him to have been a most efficient head of the police'.[31]

It was not only the metropolitan circumstances which occasioned criticism of the police. The Liverpool Cornermen brought *The Times* to accuse the Liverpool Constabulary of not being sufficiently well organised to deal with, or appreciative enough of, modern developments in the criminal world and that 'the necessity of being permanently on guard against massed brutality has not even yet been fully appreciated'.[32] The police however, withstood the criticism, largely as a result of their efficiency and professionalism, and the Home Office did not feel it necessary to inquire into the administration and organisation of the police until the Departmental Committee on the Administration and Organisation of the Metropolitan Police Force report in 1886.[33]

II

It has already been noted that the Metropolitan Police were fully aware of garotte robberies as early as 1849 and that orders were issued for officers to look out for females loitering in suspicious circumstances who may have been acting as bait for the victims of garotters. Although it was common for the public and the press to make uninformed criticism of the police as inefficient and ineffectual, a study of Police Orders during 1862 shows that the police were alert to the danger long before it came to the public notice and were taking practical steps to prevent the wave of attacks before Mr Pilkington MP, was attacked. The Police Orders were printed and issued daily and read by station sergeants to all constables prior to their commencing their duties. On 15 April 1862, William C. Harris, the Metropolitan Commissioner of Police, called for a return of all cases of robbery and theft with violence occurring in the streets during the last year.[34] On 15 July 1862, forty-eight hours before the Pilkington attack, Commissioner Richard Mayne issued the following orders:

ROBBERIES WITH VIOLENCE – Two cases of robbery, with great violence, were committed in 'C' Division last night, and one in 'F' Division[35] on the night of the 8th inst. The persons robbed were struck or attacked from behind, and some heavy instrument seems to have been used. The attention of all Serjeants and Constables of every Division on duty during the night is to be specially directed to these cases, that they may use the utmost observation and exertion to detect parties likely to commit such offences.[36]

On 16 July 1862, the police put the underworld under pressure and warned potential garotters that the police were putting them under surveillance by carrying out the following directive:

PUBLIC HOUSES TO BE VISITED BY POLICE IN PLAIN CLOTHES – Superintendents of Divisions are to arrange that all public houses of bad repute and places of resort of criminal characters may be visited between the hours of 11 at night and 2 a.m. by Police in plain clothes acquainted with the persons of those likely to commit street robberies. Such persons are to be kept under observation, as far as practicable, if they go into the streets, and the hour they are seen is to be noted.[37]

The police were under instructions from the Home Office not to harass convicts released on tickets-of-leave as this was thought to be detrimental to the convicts' prospect of gaining an honest livelihood – the main object of the ticket-of-leave system. The police, however, were more realistic in their approach and compiled lists of all persons convicted of robbery with violence and similar crimes and released on ticket-of-leave since 1 April 1862.[38] This produced a list of 61 persons. The 15 tickets-of-leave whose stated destination was within the Metropolitan Police district were subject to careful enquiry ... made quietly ... as to previous character, present course of life, associates, etc.'. The officers were warned that, 'In making this enquiry, great care is to be taken so as not to interfere with any of the persons who are gaining an honest livelihood'.[39]

On 18 July 1862, the following order was issued:

ROBBERIES IN STREETS – In reference to the cases of robbery in the streets that have recently been committed, the Police on beats at night are to make special observation on dark passages, entries, corners of squares, doorways in which a person may be concealed and rush out to commit a crime.[40]

On 14 August it was arranged that 17 sergeants and 176 constables should be employed in plain clothes to patrol from 10 p.m. to 2 a.m. They were to be the men best acquainted with bad characters and best qualified for detective duty. The were to visit public houses and known criminal haunts occasionally. Their immediate and most important duty was 'the prevention of robberies and other crimes committed with violence in the streets'.[41]

It seems quite apparent from the above that the police took prompt and effective action and that it is probably as a result of this that the number of persons committed for trial for robbery with violence increased. The press seemed largely uninformed as to the action the police took and gave them little, if any, credit. The majority of the press and the public took the rising number of committals as evidence of a crime wave and police inaction. The number of crimes committed in the

Table 6.1 Number of crimes committed and the number of persons
apprehended 1862/63

	Crimes Committed	Persons Apprehended
October, November, December	14,356	8,195
January, February, March	13,606	7,719
April, May, June	12,380	7,407
July, August, September	11,869	7,689
	52,211	30,010

Source: 'Judicial Statistics 1863', *P.P. (1864)*, LVII, 445, p. xi

winter of 1862 and the first three quarters of 1863 showed a decrease of
1,614 or 2 per cent in comparison to 1862 while the number of persons
apprehended showed an increase of 1,190 or 4 per cent,[42] which supports
the theory that the police acted efficiently. In 1863 the apprehensions
were 57.5 per cent of the number of crimes committed. This is a high
clear-up rate. (In 1982 only 37 per cent of crimes were cleared up.[43])

The November sessions of the Central Criminal Court in 1862
marked the highpoint of the establishment's offensive against the
garotters. In June 1863, Sir Richard Mayne told Lord Carnavon that
the 27 or 28 garotters who appeared before Baron Bramwell probably
accounted for nearly all the 82 robberies with violence which had
occurred in the metropolis in the last six months of 1862.[44] The *Annual
Review* for 1862 took the same view and observed that the police had
either captured all the garotters or that the sentences had intimidated
their fellow criminals as it was perceived that the violence had stopped
from that date.

III

The Metropolitan Police were responsible directly to the Home
Secretary whilst other forces were controlled by the watch committees of
local authorities. The watch committee had the power to appoint,
promote, punish, dismiss or suspend men of all ranks. It laid down the
rates of pay and the regulations of the force and was comprised of elected
town-councillors. However, it introduced an element of local political
pressure on the police which did not apply to the Metropolitan Police.

This seemed to be apparent in the two episodes of street violence in Liverpool, the Cornermen and the High Rip. The local police 'functioned as part of a local system of control and management, specifically ... as the defensive arm of local property owners, and as the administrative agency of local magistrates and watch committees'.[45] The head constable of the mid-Victorian borough identified himself with his masters and in return the watch committee's protection of a head constable was absolute, except in cases where such support could only be followed by loss of public esteem. The town councils rarely inquired closely into the work of the watch committees, whose deliberations were held in secret and were not reported in the local press.

Following the Tithebarn Street murder, Liverpool Town Council, and especially its watch committee, came under attack from all quarters of the press. Its position was made worse by the fact that the national government, in the person of the Home Secretary, had appeared to move very quickly to solve the problem of brutal assaults at national level, while local government appeared to be complacent and inactive.

Liverpool watch committee was not drawn into the Tithebarn Street murder affair until the time of the trial when the newspaper attacks became so fierce that it called for a report to repudiate the newspapers' claims. In August the chairman of the watch committee had called for a report following allegations that no police had been on duty in the area at the time of the murder. Both these reports show a completely different side to the entire episode. They give the impression of a low-class drunkard picking a fight and being accidentally killed, a police force doing its job to the best of its ability although under strength. Above all, a study of the watch committee reports places the whole affair into a perspective which the newspapers never could, and possibly, never wanted to present.

In the *Watch Committee's Orders to the Head Constable*[46] the murder is not mentioned and the major resolution passed in 1874 followed a request from the Chairman of the Arts Sub-committee for the police band to play every Saturday during the autumn exhibition of pictures. The prevalence of vandalism in the city was hinted at in a letter from A.J. Liddell, drawing the attention of the watch committee to the damage sustained by earthenware insulators on telegraph poles as a result of stone throwing.

Only on 29 February 1874 was any topic remotely connected with street violence discussed. The watch committee read a letter from the Rev. John Jones 'applying for permission to examine the "Assault Book" at Main Bridewell in order to extract the number of cases of violence for the last three months of the year'. The watch committee revealed its isolationist tendencies which so inflamed the press and resolved, 'That the application be *not* complied with'.

It is in the *Head Constable's Special Report Book*[47] that the police view of the murder is revealed. On 11 August a report was presented, 'in reference to the alleged absence of the Police in Tithebarn Street, during the time that Richard Morgan got kicked to death'. It transpired that Mr David Ellis and his wife, the tobacconists from 79, Tithebarn Street, had seen Morgan and his wife at the 'Druids Gala', New Ferry, at 5 o'clock that evening. At about 9.30 that evening Mrs Morgan bought some tobacco at the shop while her husband and brother-in-law walked on to the end of Lower Milk Street where Mr Ellis, who was putting up his shutters, heard a disturbance and saw a crowd immediately gather. The kicking lasted about five minutes and several shop-owners (tobacconists and confectioners) stated that, 'they thought it was an ordinary street brawl and therefore did not go outside to see it'. William Rayton, a publican from 73, Tithebarn Street, said he was in the bar at the time and heard nothing. From the watch committee's point of view the most important fact ascertained was that between 9.15 and 9.45 'the spot where the murder was committed was visited by the Inspector, the Acting Inspector and six police constables'.

The report compiled for the chairman of the watch committee on 4 January 1875, reflected the official presentation of the incident adopted by the town council and police policy in relation to similar incidents. The report, written in a logical and unemotive style, contrasts with the press handling of the subject, and is most convincing. One is left with the feeling that the police exercised as much control as was possible over the neighbourhood and were well organised. The main points from the report may be summarised as follows:

1. Although the Tithebarn Street incident was deplorable, 'the case is an isolated one there, and a serious case may take place in a noisy and bustling thoroughfare'. Tithebarn Street was 'an orderly place, as compared with Marybone, Standish Street and adjacent streets, nothing having occurred there either before or since' and that, except for Marybone and Scotland Place (where additional police had been sent) there had been no well-grounded complaint of ruffianism.

2. It was police practice to anticipate potential disturbances. Information was received from detective forces and other sources and additional constables were sent, for example, to Marybone on the St John's eve Roman Catholic celebration (23 June). 'More than ordinary watchfulness is paid to the mood and temper of the persons in low neighbourhoods and especially on peculiar occasions such as 17th March (St Patrick) and 12th July (Orange) – the patrols are strengthened and well held in reserve'. Faction

fights occasionally occurred in Foutway Street and these required additional constables in plain clothes, 'to stop the stone-throwing in the afternoon, with more men in uniform at night; and arrangements are always made by which additional assistance can at once be sent'.

3. The Head Constable stated that there was a great loss of police time in attending court but that the number of cases testified to police efficiency. He believed that in important cases the offenders rarely escaped. He also stated that, 'although the mere assembling at corners of streets has not hitherto been held a punishable offence, except on the grounds of obstruction, the police have full instructions to prevent any assemblage, even in small numbers; and in few cases have they been obliged to resort to compulsion'. As to the courage of his constables, he had 'never known of unwillingness on the part of constables to go into any rough neighbourhood, let the occasion be what it might'.

It must have appeared to the town council that all contingencies were covered and that Liverpool had a police force of which it could be proud and in Major Greig a Head Constable in whom it could place justified faith. The press was not convinced. *The Times* stirred up a hornet's nest with a post-trial editorial which referred to a 'stain on the good name of Liverpool which it is incumbent on her to wipe away'.[48] What incensed *The Times* was that upright, decent citizens of Liverpool had stood and watched as a fellow, upright, decent citizen had been kicked to death.

Although this scenario was a figment of *The Times*'s imagination, this was how the incident was presented to its readership and *The Times* gave advice that, 'the people of Liverpool must not allow themselves to be thought indifferent in a case which has brought disgrace on their town'. The attack on Liverpool was under way. On 26 December 1874 *The Times* declared, 'the condition of Liverpool whether from a santiary or moral point of view, is as far as possible from satisfactory'. The paper analysed the situation as being a case of increased wages leading to increased drinking, resulting in increased violence. The editors agreed that, 'crimes of violence are, indeed, committed almost as frequently in other places; but in no other large town do they occur under the same circumstances'. The difference lay in the fact that only in Liverpool were such occurrences 'both positively approved by the brutalised population of the neighbourhood at the time, and is not publicly repudiated afterwards by the civilised portion of the inhabitants'. In *The Times*'s opinion, 'Liverpool is a town whose leading inhabitants are negligent of their duties as citizens'. The police inevitably bore the brunt of the attack and *The Times* believed that if more efficient use of the existing force and a greater activity on the part of the population did not suffice, then more police should be employed and 'the expense of the change would be no unfit penalty for the blood-guiltiness of the town in the matter of Richard Morgan'. The fact that Morgan was murdered in open streets, according to *The Times*, indicated a 'gross neglect of duty' by the police. The final goad came with the observation that London had thirty times the mileage of Liverpool's streets but only ten times the police force and the conclusion that, 'the state of Liverpool must therefore be very bad indeed if the town really needs to be guarded by a larger force than at present'. Such a comment, when seen in the context of the inter-city rivalry whose prevalence has been described by Asa Briggs[49] was indeed wounding.

On 11 January 1875 *The Times* accused the Liverpool police of failing to patrol the smaller streets and courts and of confining themselves to the main thoroughfares over which they 'exercise, on the whole, a tolerably efficient protection'. The paper stated that the strictly circumscribed neglected regions were suffering a continual increase of population and the 'new arrivals have all somehow to be crowded in'. *The Times* urged that 'these squalid dens should be pulled down and proper buildings erected in their place'. *The Times*, basing itself on no real evidence and no precedence but in a tone reflecting its image as the fourth estate in the nation then proceeded to warn Liverpool that repetitions of the Tithebarn Street murder would:

> ... lead to an inquiry from the Home Office, and the question would arise whether it had not become necessary that the management of the Police of Liverpool should be transferred to other hands, which might be trusted to make better provision than Liverpool has lately known for the maintenance of public order.

Such comments did not pass unnoticed. *The Liverpool Albion* noted that the 'general community were no doubt giving their attention to the further strong comments which *The Times*, looking upon us from a distance with strict impartiality, makes', and inferred that '*The Times* seeks to impress upon those of position and influence among us that they are the persons directly responsible for the town's good name'.[50]

On 9 January the *Liverpool Mail* which had reported *in toto The Times*'s initial call for repudiation of the crime, reported the remarks of J.B. Aspinall, QC to Liverpool Borough Sessions, who warned that unless the police took action and if 'the newspapers elsewhere indulged in reflections upon the town of Liverpool' he was afraid that the central government would interfere and take the preservation of peace into their own hands. *The Times*'s influence was not enough, however. At the adjourned meeting of the town council on Tuesday 12 January 1875, Mr Picton, the leader of the Whig-radical minority, proposed the motion:

that the state of lawlessness in certain parts of the town indicated by recent outrages in Tithebarn Street and elsewhere demands immediate attention on the part of this Council; that the Watch Committee be instructed to institute a searching inquiry into the courses which have led to such a state of things, and to report to the Council thereon, and as to what measures can be adopted for the better protection of life and property in the districts in question.[51]

The motion was defeated 6:25.

Frustration with police inaction increased. 'We are once more thrown on the mercy of the watch committee, and the watch committee unfortunately is headed by a man who succeeds in flattering himself, and who endeavours to flatter others that the police force is as efficient and active a state as it need be', wrote the *Liverpool Town Crier*. 'We are inclined to think the police are more inactive than inefficient.'[52] A letter signed, 'A Member of the Fourth Estate' in the *Daily Post* stated that 'the worst thing Alderman Livingstone and Major Greig can do is to deny the existence of the chronic ruffianism which has been allowed to grow up in certain districts of Liverpool. The next worse thing is to deal with such districts in the brainless manner latterly in vogue'.[53] A letter, from an ex-policeman, stated that cornermen existed before and were put down by a sergeant and two plainclothes men going into the district and warning them. No arrests were necessary. 'It is probably asking too much to expect that the watch committee and the Head Constable will take this moderate and sensible view of their duties', lamented the *Daily Post* editor, 'they are lost in admiration of their own marvellous success in preventing processions and popular demonstration'.

The *Spectator*, marked as usual by its unemotional approach, noted that the watch committee, which was 'very bitter in its attacks on rhetorical reports', kept order in two-thirds of Liverpool very well and with a moderate force, 'but it is impossible not to perceive that the force in the other third is inadequate, that the police is insufficiently protected, and that the protection of witnesses is nearly illusory'.[54]

At the end of January the watch committee did decide to advertise for more constables and the *Liverpool Town Crier* was 'glad to notice that the force-worshipping Watch committee and Major Greig have been brought to see the error of their vain-glory in the supposed efficiency and activity of their men'.[55] In fact this was not a major departure from policy. The size of the force had been steadily increasing for some time. In mid-December the Head Constable had requested more clothing, 'the vacancies in the strength of the force having been still further reduced'.[56]

Only the *Liverpool Mail* retained loyalty to the watch committee and this is the line which probably merits the greatest sympathy. In an article which concludes, 'We ought never to shrink from championing Major Greig as one of the most sagacious head Constables in this kingdom', the editor wrote that 'Major Greig, C.B., has received scant courtesy and scanter justice at the hands of a small section of Whig-radical Town Councillors and prejudiced journalists'.

And there it all stopped. Cornermen suddenly became unnewsworthy. The watch committee and Major Greig attended to their duties as before and Liverpool continued to grow both in prosperity and squalor.

IV

Twelve years later local politics caused the provincial press to focus on the initial deviance of the High Rip. In 1874 the watch committee had been attacked for stubbornly refusing to increase police strength. What gave the High Rip episode the basis for being a political issue was the fact that in August 1886 the watch committee had decided to increase the police strength by sixty-five, at considerable cost to the ratepayer. Each additional constable would cost £82.15.0 per annum and each sergeant £99.9.0, of which half was covered by a Treasury grant. The Head Constable, Capt. Nott-Bower, explained that the city was very much under-policed and that the extra police would be utilised for strengthening old beats rather than for newly-created beats. The average number of beats left vacant each day had been eighty-four, caused by 'the *constantly increasing* demands of persons for the special services of Constables on particular occasions'.[57] Nott-Bower stated that, 'Liverpool is very moderately "Policed" at present as compared with other large Seaport Towns' and that if an equal number of police walking the streets to that in other towns was required an increase of 450 men would be necessary. He appended the table here entitled Table 6.2.

In a later report Nott-Bower commented, 'Were it generally known what the available strength is, the wonder would not be that a Constable is not always on the spot when he is wanted, but rather that he is so frequently there as he is'.[58]

At the Liverpool Assizes for July 1886, Mr Justice Smith commented that the calendar was 'certainly light both in quality and quantity'.[59] Whether this reflects a quiet Liverpool or an inactive police force is impossible to say. It is a fact that he said it and in this episode hard facts

Table 6.2 Strength of police in various towns

	Population 1885	Strength of Police	No. of Police per 100,000
Liverpool	579,724	981	169
London	5,147,727	14,258	277
Glasgow	519,965	1,068	205
Dublin	353,082	975	276

Source: *Head Constable's Special Report*, 30 August 1886, Liverpool Record Office, 352 Pol 2/10

were not easily uncovered, for the High Rip were classic mythical folk devils and in the end the newspaper debate which split along party lines had turned on whether the High Rip existed or not. It was the *Daily Post* and its intrepid commissioner that led the literary assault on the watch committee and attempted to convince its readership of the existence of the High Rip, thus proving the inefficiency of the police despite their expensive increase in numbers. On 20 October 1886, Capt. Nott-Bower sent a memorandum to the Chairman of the watch committee[60] in which he acknowledged the allegations of a 'Liverpool paper' and summarised them as being:

1. The existence of a conspiracy for assault and plunder organised as a secret society known as the High Rip Gang.
2. That the inhabitants of the North end are subject to assaults which are increasing in number and severity owing to the activities of the High Rip and the incompetence of the police.

The first of these allegations he categorically denied, stating in his report that, 'No conspiracy of such a character exists, save in the imagination of Newspaper Correspondents'. As to the second allegation, he stated that the statistics refuted the allegation. His annual report for the year ending 29 September 1886 showed a total of 243 indictable assaults 'which is rather below the average', and summary assaults had fallen from 1968 to 1898, 'a number far below the average of the last ten years'. It may be argued, quite correctly, that the distribution of these offences over time is not shown, but figures from Liverpool Sessions and Assizes shown in Table 6.3 for 1886 do not show any significant 'bunching' to indicate a sudden conspiracy. The police case was

Table 6.3 Cases appearing before Liverpool Sessions and Assizes for 1886

Sessions Court	No. Tried	Street violence	Per cent	Non-acquisitive violence	Robbery
February	77	13	16.9	13	
March	70	10	14.3	10	
May	81	15	18.5	15	
June	12	1	8.3	1	
July	126	21	16.7	21	
August	51	5	9.8	5	
October	95	21	22.1	21	
December	54	7	13.0	7	
Assizes					
February	74	11	14.9	4	7
May	110	31	28.2	26	5
July	98	11	11.2	8	3
November	114	24	21.0	13	11

Source: *Criminal Registers*, P.R.O. HO/27

strengthened by the fact that for the 243 indictable offences committed, 225 people had been apprehended. This figure necessarily exaggerates the achievement as several persons may have been apprehended for one offence, but it is still impressive.

Nott-Bower, having answered the allegations, proceeded to go on to the offensive against the *Daily Post* and appended some letters, 'shewing the manner in which this subject has been presented to the Public'.

The main letter was from Robert Watt, agent for Carver and Company, Carriers, of Dale Street who had written to the *Daily Post* on 22 September concerning the High Rip, as follows:

> That some idle youths do call themselves by this name may be true but they are an insignificant lot such as our Police can easily deal with and quite unworthy of the notice taken in yours of 20th. I think your representative has much overstated the case for my stables are off Vauxhall Road near to Athol Street, and on the spot he calls the 'Happy Hunting ground of the Gang' yet I have gone to and from them at all hours of the day and night for these twenty years and have not been interfered with nor have I had complaint from any of my men . . .

> Boiler Scalers and Classical Sweeps have a dirty job and I fear their black
> appearance sometimes gets them a black name, and whilst some may be
> vicious and belong to this gang they are in general not worse than other
> youths with the same upbringing.

Needless to say the letter was not printed in the *Daily Post* and Watt
wrote to the editor on 29 September to say that as his facts were not
appreciated and 'as there is always two sides to a story I have sent a copy
of my letter to the Watch committee'. Although one suspects that Watt's
motive was probably that of endearing himself to the authorities and
ensuring the renewal of his carrier's licence rather than for a desire for
the facts to be known, the letters are evidence of the selectivity of the
press in their choice of which facts to publish and which to suppress.[61]

The *Daily Post*, perhaps unaware of the sting in the tail of the report,
had certainly foreseen the gist of it and pre-empted anything it might say
with an article on 21 September. Its analysis of the situation is most
interesting and may be more appropriately applied to other panics than
to this one. On 20 September the paper stated that, 'Something must be
done to check these outrages, and it rests with the Watch committee and
the Chiefs of the Police force to devise some effectual plan'. On 21
September it repeated that, 'In the matter of the High Rip Gang, we
cannot altogether acquit the Watch committee and the Chief Constable
of a certain remissness. Its very existence is their sufficient indictment',
and went on:

> What we rather expect – for such are the ways of departments – is that the
> Watch committee will, in the first place, take refuge in contemptuous
> silence, or, if they speak up at all, talk much of the untrustworthiness of
> anonymous statements. The next step, if the controversy is kept up – as in
> case of need we intend that it shall be – will be to declare that the story is
> exaggerated out of all semblance of the truth. It is only after that stage has
> been reached that we expect inquiry, and, after inquiry, some more of less
> energetic action.

This scenario, quite realistic for the metropolitan panics, was acted out
in Liverpool but without the envisaged finale. Letters and editorials
calling for action on the part of the police built up until 21 October. Law
and order had become a large election issue owing to the 'Belfast-like
rioting' in the Toxteths (South end) of the City between Catholics and
Orangemen in mid-September.[62] The *Echo* and the *Daily Post* kept up a
constant attack on the town council, accusing it of extravagance and
incompetence on a variety of issues.

Following the elections, the next focal point was the November

Assize, presided over by Sir John Day, who had just returned from Ireland, where he had 'got to the bottom – if there be one – of Belfast Ruffianism'. 'Will he do a similar service for Liverpool?' asked the *Echo*.[63]

Mr Justice Day heard the case of a man named John McShane who had shot someone in the foot after firing to disperse a crowd of High Rippers, and pronounced that he would not think it possible that such gangs existed or that there were districts where a police escort was necessary or where one needed to fire a revolver to disperse a crowd and that if that was the case it was a great discredit to the police.[64] When the stabbing case involving a dispute between the Logwood and the High Rip gangs brought two sentences of fifteen years penal servitude, the *Echo* began to interpret this as a judicial pronouncement on the shortcomings of the police force. 'Terrible as that penalty is, it is not a day too long for the personal outrage inflicted and the principle involved. Do the police still intend to ignore these "gangs", save when their victims are stabbed and left for dead in the streets'.[65] The moral entrepreneurs felt they had at last found a folk hero. On 12 November Mr Justice Day let it be known that he would tour the city and decide for himself the situation as regards the High Rip. The *Echo* could hardly contain its assumed righteousness.

> Official cognisance has been taken by Sir John C. Day, her Majesty's Judge of Assize, and other legal personages of the existence of the High Rip gang in Liverpool. It remains for the Watch committee, or, failing that body, the City Council, to obtain an explanation of the report recently made by the Head Constable.[66]

The *Echo*, however, had been premature. That evening Mr Justice Day was taken by Nott-Bower on a midnight tour of the city. Two detectives, Nott-Bower, Day and Mr Justice Grantham toured the Scotland district for two or three hours. The judges admitted that what they saw was a revelation to them and Day was later to make a similar tour with Mr Justice Wills. Day, who was a close friend of Nott-Bower, was faced with about twenty cases of robbery with violence which he kept back to the last day for sentencing. He gave 20 to 30 lashes each to be administered in two instalments, the second just prior to release.[67] On closing the Sessions on 19 November, Day pronounced:

> There may be found in Liverpool as in every large town, a very large number of ruffians who do indulge in vice and ruffiansim ... I have never seen and cannot believe that there is anything in Liverpool of the nature of

an organisation of ruffians banded together against the law. All I say is that there may be, but I have seen no evidence of it.[68]

The *Daily Post* later summarised Day's remarks as a 'statement to the effect that it was all idle talk'.[69] The *Echo* rationalised its position by pursuing a semantic argument that Day admitted that ruffians existed in bands but did not know them by the name of High Rippers and consoled themselves with the fact that, 'when Mr Justice Day's "ruffians" are caged, the High Rippers will not be at large'.[70] In early March the city council discussed the subject but 'didn't throw much light on the subject' and Alderman John Hughes stated that inquiries were being made.[71]

The reputation of the police remained unscathed and it was perhaps that of the newspapers which was tarnished as a result of the High Rip episode. The Metropolitan Police did not fare so well following the ruffianism of the Trafalgar Square meeting of the same year. It was little wonder that the national newspapers did not choose the High Rip as an excuse for a comparison of the Metropolitan and Liverpool forces as they had done with the Cornermen.

V

A rally of the unemployed had been called for Monday, 8 February 1886 by the 'London United Workmen's Committee'. On 2 February the LUWC arranged for a deputation to meet the Metropolitan Police Commissioner and, in accordance with normal procedure, the Chief Commissioner, E.Y.W. Henderson called for reports from all divisions as to where the marchers would assemble and the estimated numbers attending. The next day the LUWC wrote to clarify the fact that they were not associated with the 'Social Democratic Confederation' but that 'they were a body of hardworking, peaceable men, who intended to conduct their meeting with moderation and with temperate language'.[72] However, on 5 February socialist notices appeared in newspapers urging followers to seize the platform of the LUWC. Foreseeing trouble, the Chief Commissioner put 563 policemen of all ranks in reserve near Trafalgar Square in addition to the sixty-six constables on duty in the Square itself. At noon on Monday the Chief Commissioner, in an interview with the new Home Secretary, Childers, assured him that he had detailed what he believed 'to be a sufficient number of the police force to maintain order in the Square itself, and had given the necessary orders for the protection of property along the lines of the route by which the crowds were expected to march'. The Commissioner later explained to the Committee of Inquiry that he did not make other arrangements for the protection of property as in his experience such crowds always dispersed by the same route along which they had marched. Unfortunately for Henderson, this was the exception that proved the rule.

The police later stated that 'the meeting itself, though composed of very rough elements who indulged in a certain amount of horse-play, was not a disorderly one'.[73] It was large but not massive and its containment was well within the capabilities of the Metropolitan Police force. Some thirteen years earlier the *Westminster Review* had explained that 'as the commissioners command the whole district, and the force is organised and united, while roughs act in small areas, and have diverse and selfish interests, the peace of London may be held secure against violence'.[74] For the politically aware, it probably showed the divisions in the socialist ranks rather than a cohesive party marching towards one goal, so that from a political point of view this demonstration can have caused little alarm to the establishment. What the establishment feared was the rough element of society, following an anti-government leadership. At 4 p.m. they were reminded that the rough element without leadership and out of control in the geographical areas which were assumed to be the domain of the propertied classes could bring more concretely-based fear to persons who unhappily found themselves on the spot.

The *Morning Post* believed that many of the roughs had armed themselves with brickbats and stones in advance as the wooden pavements of Pall Mall, St James's Street, Piccadilly and Oxford Street would not provide them with ammunition.[75] When the window-breaking started the police faced a charge-of-the-light-brigade situation. The Commissioner saw the danger at 4 p.m. and sent a message to the superintendent in charge of one hundred reserves to go to Pall Mall. This message was mis-communicated with the result that the one hundred reserves were rushed to The Mall and protected the unthreatened Buckingham Palace. If the message had been correctly communicated it is likely that the riot would have been averted and the meeting would have paled into insignificance as just another Trafalgar Square meeting. In fact the meeting would have been placed in the right historical perspective.

The Commissioner was severely criticised for arrangements which were 'most unsatisfactory and very defective in their conception' and for failure to take action on the day, 'although it was well understood that a large element of a very dangerous class was present'.[76] The publication of the Committee of Inquiry's findings led to the announcement by the Home Secretary, on 23 February 1886, of an Inquiry into the Administration and Organisation of the Metropolitan Police Force. The report of this inquiry[77] recommended changes in the use of the telegraphic system; the positioning of superior officers at demonstrations; the use of mounted police; the chain of responsibility; the police regulations for dealing with large meetings and the system of communications with the Home Office. The first real test of the new procedures came at the large socialist meeting in Trafalgar Square on 13 November 1887, known in socialist circles as 'Bloody Sunday'. One thousand, seven hundred police were on duty inside the square while two squadrons of Life Guards – 'the river of steel and scarlet' – cleared the Strand in a 'brief but fiery struggle' and Alfred Linnel died in hospital as a result of injuries received from the police.

Reviewing letters to *The Times* following the 1886 incident, E.P. Thompson[78] notes that worse riots had occurred in most years in some parts of the country but not on such sanctified ground as Pall Mall. It was when the roughs preyed upon the middle classes or encroached into middle-class areas that the newspapers valued them as good material with which to scare their middle-class readership which paid the police rates. The police, who by mid-century had become far more professional and well-organised than most of the readership suspected, then became the butt for much of the criticism, much of which was unfounded and often based on imaginary visions of the good old days. Thompson quotes a letter which was in the firm disciplinary mode from Wilbraham Taylor, published on 11 February 1886, when the general feeling was that the police had demonstrated great weakness in Trafalgar Square.

Sir,
On returning from the Prince's Levee I was walking through Pall Mall, in uniform. It was gradually filling with very suspicious-looking 'unemployed' at that time, two of whom, turning towards me, one said, rather significantly, 'Why who the _____ is this chap?'
As I passed the War Office entrance, formerly the Duke of Buckingham's, a blind fiddler, led by a little girl came by ... playing some odd tune or other, when a young guardsman on sentry stepped out and said in a commanding tone, 'You stop that noise' ... I thought, 'Now there is a man of common sense and action'. It was a little thing to stop at the time but when the snowball which a child or a blind fiddler could set rolling on the top of the hill, reaches the bottom it has become in this country an immovable monster, in other countries a destroying avalache.
On 10th April 1848, I was sworn in as special constable between Buckingham Palace and the House of Commons. At the former we had a

battery of Horse Artillery hidden in the stable yard. I asked the officer commanding what he was going to do? His answer was, 'We have our scouts and if we hear of any gatherings we could run out and sweep the Mall or the Birdcage Walk in two minutes or command St. James' Street or Pall Mall in three'. He would not wait till mischief was done. Are these days quite gone?

It is difficult for the modern mind to understand how the leading newspaper of the time could publish such a letter, but such views, expressed in such pompous ways were most influential, and reveal that much of *The Times*'s readership wished the police to exercise a greater degree of social control. William Morris's description of Bloody Sunday, which he attended, in his *News from Nowhere* (1890), shows that such days had not quite gone and had been revived following the moral panic of 1886.

VI

Howard Jones has noted that 'the police are not unresponsive to public pressure' and if there is perceived to be a rise in criminality 'there is a tendency for them to become more severe'.[79] The newspapers in Victorian society were probably the main form of 'public pressure' but were not always first to perceive the rise in criminality. In 1862 the police had begun to take action against street robbers before the initial deviance of the attack on Pilkington. In Liverpool in 1874 the police and watch committee had been aware that they were under strength for some time and had been recruiting. Perhaps newspaper pressure speeded up the recruitment drive but this was not a major departure from police policy. In the case of the High Rip in Liverpool in 1886 there was little that the police could do other than carry out their duties as before, as they were aware that trouble from a gang of youths was not a new phenomenon, as the newspapers supposed, but a perpetual problem which was all part of the job for the police in any major city. The aftermath of the Trafalgar Square demonstration did highlight a weakness in police procedure which was acknowledged by a Committee of Inquiry and steps were taken to remedy it. On the whole the police seemed to view the panics as newspaper-fomented scares which in their professional opinion were not a result of extraordinary circumstances and therefore did not require extraordinary action. In a moral panic the first recipient of blame is always the police and it seems that the police did little to deflect the adverse publicity they received. In contrast with the media-conscious chief constables of the 1980s, it was the silence of men like Greig and Nott-Bower which infuriated the press who interpreted it as arrogance and complacency. One is left with the impression that the police were professionals who were concerned with actual criminal acts and their prevention, and not with popular myths resulting from newspaper publicity. The police were not public figures susceptible to public pressure but the legislators and judiciary were, and it is to the effect of the panics on them that our attention must now turn.

Notes

1. R. Lane, 'Crime and Criminal Statistics in Nineteenth-Century Massachusetts', *Journal of Social History*, 1968, 2, 156–63.
2. See R.D. Storch, 'The Policeman as Domestic Missionary: Urban Discipline and Popular Culture in Northern England, 1850–80', *Journal of Social History*, 1976, 9, 4, 481–509.
3. 'The Police System of London', *Edinburgh Review*, July 1852, 1–33.
4. 'The Police of London', *Quarterly Review*, 129, 1870, 87–130.
5. R.D. Storch, 'The Plague of Blue Locusts: Police Reform and Popular Resistance in Northern England, 1840–57', *International Review of Social History*, XX, 1975, 61–90.
6. R.D. Storch, 'Police Control of Street Prostitution in Victorian London: A Study in the Contexts of Police Action', in D.H. Bailey, *Police and Society* (1977).
7. Letter from 'G.W.C.', *The Times*, 3 December 1885.
8. J. Greenwood, *The Seven Curses of London* (1869), 2.
9. C. Emsley, *Policing and its Context, 1750–1870* (1983).
10. R. Roberts, *The Classic Slum: Salford Life in the First Quarter of the Century* (Manchester, 1971), 71, quoted by Storch, op.cit. (1975).
11. Storch, op.cit. (1975).
12. Report from the Select Committee on the Police of the Metropolis, P.P. (1834), xvi, q. 166.
13. Charles Dickens the Younger, *London Guidebook for 1879* (1879, reprinted 1972), 207.
14. *Punch*, 6 September 1856.
15. *Punch*, 14 February 1857.
16. C. Steedman, *Policing the Victorian Community: The Formation of English Provincial Police Forces, 1856–80* (1984).
17. Letter from 'XY', *The Times*, 31 October 1856.
18. Letter from 'Anti-Garotter', *The Times*, 11 November 1856.
19. Letter from 'One who has a great objection to being garotted', *The Times*, 31 October 1856.
20. Letter from 'G.C.', *The Times*, 24 November 1856.
21. Letter from 'Constant Reader', *The Times*, 3 November 1856.

22. *The Times*, 18 November 1856.
23. *Daily News*, 18 July 1862.
24. *The Times*, 5 November 1862.
25. *The Times*, 7 November 1862.
26. *The Times*, 28 November 1862.
27. *The Times*, 7 November 1862.
28. *Illustrated Times*, 3 January 1863.
29. Letter from 'L', *The Times*, 13 December 1843.
30. *The Times*, 4 February 1869.
31. Op.cit., *Quarterly Review*, 1870..
32. *The Times*, 30 November 1877.
33. *P.P.*, c. 4894.
34. *Metropolitan Police Orders*, 15 April 1862, P.R.O. M/Pol 7/14.
35. 'C' Division was the St James's Division based at Little Vine Street, Piccadilly. 'F' Division was the Holborn Division based at Bow Street, Tottenham Court Road and Brunswick Square.
36. *Metropolitan Police Orders*, 15 July 1862, P.R.O. M/Pol 7/14.
37. *Metropolitan Police Orders*, 16 July 1862, P.R.O. M/Pol 7/14.
38. *Metropolitan Police Orders*, 18 July 1862, P.R.O. M/Pol 7/14.
39. *Metropolitan Police Orders*, 4 August 1862, P.R.O. M/Pol 7/14.
40. *Metropolitan Police Orders*, 18 July 1862, P.R.O. M/Pol 7/14.
41. *Metropolitan Police Orders*, 14 August 1862, P.R.O. M/Pol 7/14.
42. *Judicial Statistics*, 1863, P.P. (1864) LVII, 445, p.xi.
43. *Criminal Statistics: England and Wales 1982*, P.P. (1983) c. 9048, 38.
44. House of Lords Report, *The Times*, 10 June 1863.
45. Steedman, op.cit., 5.
46. Liverpool Record Office, 352, Pol 1/13.
47. Liverpool Record Office, 352, Pol 2/6.
48. *The Times*. 17 December 1874.
49. A. Briggs, *Victorian Cities* (1963).
50. *Liverpool Albion*, 12 January 1875.
51. *Liverpool Mail*, 16 January 1875.
52. *Liverpool Town Crier*, 16 January 1875.
53. *Daily Post*, 18 January 1875.
54. *Spectator*, 16 January 1875.
55. *Liverpool Town Crier*, 30 January 1875.
56. *Watch Committee Orders to the Head Constable*, 15 December 1874.
57. *Head Constable's Special Report*, 30 August 1886, Liverpool Record Office 352 Pol 2/10.
58. *Head Constable's Special Report*, 15 February 1887, Liverpool Record Office 352 Pol 2/10.
59. *Liverpool Daily Post*, 29 July 1886.
60. *Head Constable's Special Report*, 20 October 1886, Liverpool Record Office 352 Pol 2/10.
61. The selection of letters for publication is an interesting process. At present *The Times* receives an average of 200 letters per day. Each is entered in a

register which is kept for 12–18 months. *The Times* appointed its first letter editors in 1922. Letters are chosen for publication on the basis of 'newsworthyness, quality of expression, topicality and similar consideration'. The *Daily Telegraph* rejects about 90 per cent of the letters received. The correspondence editor is 'looking for letters which are interesting and/or help to provide a balance to something that has happened previously in the paper'. Private correspondence to author from Times Newspapers Ltd., 16 January 1984 and the *Daily Telegraph*, 11 January 1984.

62. *Liverpool Echo*, 20 September 1886.
63. *Liverpool Echo*, 11 November 1886.
64. *Liverpool Echo*, 8 November 1886.
65. *Liverpool Echo*, 12 November 1886.
66. *Liverpool Echo*, 13 November 1886.
67. Sir William Nott-Bower, *Fifty-Two Years a Policeman* (1926), 150; Arthur Day, *John C.F.S. Day* (1916), 119.
68. *Liverpool Echo*, 20 November 1886.
69. *Liverpool Daily Post*, 1 March, 1887.
70. *Liverpool Echo*, 20 November 1886.
71. *Liverpool Review*, 5 March 1887.
72. 'Disturbances (Metropolis): Report from the Committee on the Recent Disturbances and the Conduct of the Police Authority', *P.P. (1886)*, c. 4665, vol. xxxiv p.iii. Much of the following account is taken from this source.
73. Evidence of E.Y. W. Henderon, Commissioner of Police, ibid., 94.
74. 'The Metropolitan Police System', *Westminster Review*, January 1873, 16.
75. *Morning Post*, 9 February 1886.
76. 'Disturbances (Metropolis)', p.vi–vii.
77. *Report of the Inquiry into the Administration and Organisation of the Metropolitan Police Force* (1886), c. 4894, vol.XXXIV.
78. E.P. Thompson, 'Sir, Writing by Candlelight', *New Society*, 24 December 1970, 1135–36.
79. H. Jones, *Crime in a Changing Society* (1965), 12.

7. *The Effect of the Panics on the Legislature*

I

The major test of a moral panic is whether it resulted in panic legislation and such panic legislation as a reaction to one particular event was not uncommon in Britain's long parliamentary history. Sir J.F. Stephen described, in 1877, how the splitting of Sir William Coventry's nose as an act of revenge led to an Act (22 and 23 Car. 2 c.1) which made it a felony to split people's noses. The Black Acts (9 Geo. 1 c.22) making it a felony to inflict various specified kinds of bodily injury resulted from the actions of a band of deerstealers on Waltham Chase called the Waltham Blacks from their habit of blacking their faces. Stephen also mentions the Garotting Act of 1863 and notes that 'it is in this piecemeal manner that our statute law on the subject of crime has grown up'.[1] G.R. Scott notes that 'the laws relating to corporal punishment have invariably been enacted in states of panic or under the influence of deep unreasoning emotion'.[2] As examples he cites the clause in the Treason Act of 1842 providing for whipping as a penalty for aiming a firearm at a sovereign following the public outcry when the life of Queen Victoria was threatened, the Garotting Act occasioned by the 1862 epidemic and the provisions for the whipping of procurers and pimps in the Criminal Law Amendment Act of 1912 following the panic occasioned by the prevalence of reports of 'white slave' trafficking at that time. Howard Jones, commenting on the outbreaks of crime, observes that 'perhaps the greater danger is that we may be panicked into measures of repression which will do more damage to our system of values than the crime itself'.[3] The main effect of the moral panics of the nineteenth century was the resulting legislation concerning the penal system.

II

The ticket-of-leave man 'has at length succeeded in moving the masses, and the masses will come down on his head and crush him'.

Blackwood's Edinburgh Magazine, Vol. 81, February 1857

We cannot but congratulate the country at large on the assault committed on the HON. MR. LILLIPUT: for as the Hon. gentleman is nephew to a Duke, brother-in-law to a Marquess, cousin to an Earl, a Duchess and a Bishop, and further, is about to be allied to the daughter of an ex-chancellor, there can be no doubt that at length, the crying, killing evil of the ticket-of-leave system will be put down with a strong hand. Of course, vulgar assaults we must, from time to time, always expect: but when the Garotte enters the bosom of a nobleman's family, it is high time for the laws to better themselves.

Punch, 6 December 1856

In 1852 the system of transportation to Australia, which had commenced in 1787 to supplement the hulks, was abolished under pressure of Australian public opinion. Britain, therefore, had quickly to find a way to deal with her own convicts on her own shores.

In the 1840s three systems of discipline in prison were current and formed the subject for debate. Under the Silent System prisoners were not allowed to communicate, wearing hoods when exercising. The system had gained popular support from the press and prison authorities and had been widely adopted as it needed no new building. It attracted criticism as the system required such harsh discipline as to make reformation impossible.

The Separate System, aimed at the prevention of moral contamination through mixing, required the building of new cellular prisons. The completely new model prison at Pentonville commenced in 1840 and the massive cellular penitentiary constructed at Perth to serve the whole of Scotland in 1842 marked a quiet revolution in penal reform. Attitudes towards and the treatment of the prisoner within the Separate System was still a matter of great public debate. Much of this debate was based on the efficacy or otherwise of the Mark System, formulated by Captain Maconochie. Under this system the prisoner earned marks for good conduct (as a sign of reform) and required a certain number of marks to obtain his release. Maconochie was appointed Governor of Birmingham Gaol in 1849 and introduced a version of the Mark System based on various grades of discipline ranging from crank labour in solitary cells to easy employment in the workshops or garden. Birmingham ratepayers found the system too soft and called for common sense and the treadmill rather than the benevolent experiments. Maconochie was dismissed.

The 'Criminal Question' as the press entitled this public debate consisted by this time of three strands. First, there was an increasing need for new prisons to be built in Britain and an awareness that the old system was not efficient. Secondly, there was a constant pressure from a small but influential group of liberal-minded prison reformers to better prison conditions and to concentrate on the reforming rather than deterrent aspects of prison discipline. Finally there was the strand of public opinion which was not constant. From the beginning of the century until the late 1840s public opinion was silent on the matter and the prison system was gradually made more humane without receiving too much publicity. Public opinion began to change when it was felt that the new trends in prison systems were not producing the required results. This change in public opinion is not easy to account for. Public opinion tended at one and the same time to be moulded and reflected by the press. The press seemed to decide that crime committed by unreformed prisoners was on the increase and highlighted this by reporting such crimes in greater numbers. The press increased their reports and comment on violent burglaries in 1850 and on street violence, to some extent in 1853 and noticeably in 1856 and 1862–3 and these reports coincided with the formulation of policy which led to the Penal Servitude Act of 1853, the Select Committees on Transportation of 1856 and 1863 and the Prisons Act of 1865.

Maconochie's dismissal was closely tied up with the progress that public opinion was making with regard to the 'Criminal Question'. The controversy over prison discipline revived in 1847 and William Clay assessed the turn of events in the following revealing manner:

> By degrees, almost the whole press, which had been generally favourable to the plan of separation in 1847, veered round into brisk hostility. Early in 1849 *The Times* began to fulminate: presently the *Daily News*, with other newspapers, took part (though with mitigated vehemence) in the attack. And of course their 'facetious contemporary', follow-my-leader *Punch*, immediately flung his squibs at the unpopular system.[4]

However, it was not only the press which turned against the 'soft' systems. Carlyle wrote *Model Prisons* and Dickens, who had already criticised the Philadelphia system in his *American Notes* (1842) wrote the final instalment of *David Copperfield* in which Uriah Heep, deeply 'umble, took leave in the character of a model prisoner.

In the early 1850s a series of violent burglaries was widely reported in the press and several reformers seized this opportunity to put forward new plans. The Mark System was proposed by Matthew Davenport-Hill, the Recorder of Birmingham but this 'excited tremendous opposition'. The Davenport-Hills argue, however, that eventually the action of criminals especially garotters and burglars, proved the need for a new system which was introduced by the Penal Servitude Act of 1853; 'burglaries and garottings brought the nation to acquiesce in the soundness of Mr Hill's proposal'.[5] In the spring of 1853 parliamentary debate on the system of transportation had become more and more heated. In 1847 the Committee of the House of Lords had come out 'very strongly against the abolition of the system of transporting offenders'.[6] The scheme then in use was that offenders were punished in Britain, first by separate confinement and then by employment on public works and ultimately they were removed on a ticket of leave to the colonies. With the discovery of gold in Australia this ticket of leave was worth the effort of conducting oneself in accordance with the wishes of the prison authorities. Suddenly, in 1853, the removal of convicts to Van Dieman's land (Tasmania) ceased and the numbers sent to Western Australia had to be drastically curtailed. Lord Aberdeen told the House that the government was considering releasing in Britain the 1,052 convicts at Portland, Dartmoor, Gibraltar and Bermuda who were due a ticket of leave.[7]

Lord Grey intimated that if anyone had seen the effect of a returned convict on a country parish the proposed bill would not receive the Royal Assent. He argued that in country districts returned convicts brought mischief and danger. They seduced the young into crime, taught them that punishment was not terrible and showed them the best and newest methods of committing crime. 'In short, his presence was a sort of moral pollution'.[8] Lord Grey's warnings were to no avail. The Penal Servitude Act of 1853 received the Royal Assent on 20 August 1853. It was this Act and its maladministration which the public mind was to blame for all garotte outbreaks thereafter.

The Act introduced the principle of the Mark System by allowing any ticket-of-leave man to be recommitted if found associating with bad characters, leading an idle or dissolute life or with no visible means of obtaining an honest livelihood. In theory a prisoner's conduct determined his discharge, but in practice the Act was marked by maladministration and its provisions were never fully carried out.

The Times was the main perpetrator of the myth that 'the ticket-of-leave men are ever foremost in these garotte robberies, as in other crimes',[9] although during the panic of 1856 a barrister pointed out to readers of The Times that as sentences of penal servitude were for a minimum of four years, 'no one at that time could have been realeased on a ticket-of-leave issued under the 1853 Act'.[10]

In the winter of 1855 Sir Joshua Jebb (the Director of Prisons) felt it necessary to write to The Times on what was felt to be 'unquestionably one of the most important social questions of the present day'.[11] It is a measure of the power of the press that they had made it one of the most important social questions of the day and that the Director of Prisons used the medium of the press to put across his message to the public. Jebb felt that 'the want of accurate information had been the cause of the misapprehension which exists'.[12] He maintained that since 8 October 1853, 3,629 licences had been issued and only 96 (2.75 per cent) had been revoked and concluded that although any relapse into crime was regrettable it was a 'matter for surprise it is the very small proportion that have done so'. The press and the public evidently did not agree with Jebb's conclusion, for in December 1855 he wrote again to *The Times* that, 'a very wrong impression of it [the system] has been created and still exists in the public mind'.[13] Jebb argued that the press were not only being unfair in their reports but were helping to fulfil their own gloomy prophecies by alarming people into not employing released prisoners on licence who had then little alternative than to resort to crime in order to obtain a living. The public should be given facts so that they could form an opinion, rather than 'be left in such a state of alarm as is absolutely creating the very dangers which have been apprehended', Jebb wrote, 'by depriving the men of the means of obtaining employment'. He assured the public that no man was released on licence on the say of the prison chaplain (a common complaint in the press) and that regular records of conduct and work were kept by different and independent officers.

The furore was enough to force the formation of a Select Committee on Transportation in 1856. Some newspapers would not accept the reality of the situation which forced transportation to end as a punishment and believed it was entirely as a result of soft humanitarian reformers. The *Morning Chronicle* admitted that, 'We cannot pollute our free colonies with the very dregs and off-scourings of our own society', but wondered, 'may we not offer them, and will they refuse to entertain, the *best* of our convicts'.[14] The *Daily News* was more willing to accept the inevitable. Although they entirely concurred with the Select Committee on Transportation's first resolution, 'That the punishment of transportation is more effectual and deterring, better adapted for the ultimate reformation of convicts, and more beneficial to this country, than any other secondary punishment for serious crimes which has yet been tried'[15] they were quick to conclude, a few days later, that, 'a revival cannot reasonably be looked forward to as a practical resource for disposing of the great bulk of more serious offenders'.[16] This point was gradually accepted and established in the public mind. The Select Committee on Transportation did not aid the establishment of this fact as it recommended 'the continutation of the sentence of transportation, as far as Her Majesty's dominions may afford safe and proper facilities for that purpose' but as the *Daily News* noted, the real question was how far the dominions did afford such facilities and that on this point 'the resolutions of the Committee are silent'. The *Morning Chronicle* revealed the feeling of frustration and helplessness that was causing the alarm and despondency throughout the country. As with the majority of public opinion the paper was opposed to the ticket-of-leave system system and the new humanitarian approach to prison reform but could offer nothing constructive with which to replace it, except criticism of the authorities and wild forecasts of the imminent downfall of the ticket-of-leave system. In December the editor wrote:

> Public sentiment revolts against hanging the criminals in sufficient numbers to act as a salutory warning. Politico-economists denounce the profitable employment of the prisoners as an interference with the rights of labour; and they condemn life imprisonment. In Heaven's name, then, what is to be done with the criminal? One thing is perfectly clear, he must not be longer permitted in the guise of a 'ticket-of-leave' man, to lay waste and desolate, to garotte and plunder his unoffending and well-disposed countrymen. The system has been tried and found wanting. Philanthropists and prison reformers, the days of your latest pet theory are numbered.[17]

The reformers, who had tried and were now adjudged to have failed, were the main object of attack in this outburst of national frustration. An article written on Christmas Eve 1856, appearing in *Blackwood's Edinburgh Magazine* stated that it was not sorry 'for the panic and its causes as it served to explode the bubble of human perfectibility and turn people against the humanity lobby'. Many now agreed that there were 'worse remedies for moral disease than honest hanging'.[18] It was almost with righteous joy that the more conservative and reactionary organs of the press, in their role as moral entrepreneurs, viewed the failure of prison reform. The *Morning Chronicle* noted that garotting and murderous assault were increasing rapidly at a time 'when the country is congratulating itself upon the moral and educational advances which it has made'. This had left philanthropists sorely puzzled and the theorisers on the perfectibility utterly bewildered as they saw, 'one after another, the utter failure of their schemes for reforming the criminal'.[19]

By mid-December the *Morning Chronicle* accurately reflected the vast majority of public opinion in writing that while the controversies concerning abstract questions went on, 'society in general has arrived at its own practical determination'. The feeling of alarm inspired by garotting had delivered a *coup de grace* to the system so 'there must be no more tickets of leave. That is decided'.[20] However, it was far from decided. The small section of informed opinion prevailed. The Select Committee of the House of Commons appointed to consider alternatives to the ticket-of-leave system heard the evidence, and, although bemoaning the end of transportation facilities previously made available by the colonies, found the principles on which the ticket-of-leave system were founded to be sound and decided that the system should be persevered with. Horatio Waddington, Under-Secretary of State at the Home Office, in evidence to the Select Committee inquiring into the working of the 1853 Act, noted that in England and Wales in 1854 there had actually been a diminution in highway robbery.[21] The committee's findings were made law by the Penal Servitude Act of 1857 (20–21 Vict. c.3). Much of the slack administration of the 1853 Act was tightened up and on 27 June 1857, Sir George Grey issued a circular to explain how the Act was to work. However, it was true that all convicts were still released after the shortest legal period and that police 'supervision during the remitted period was entirely given up'.[22]

The situation was still far from perfect and although there was a lull in the debate the basis of the next panic in 1862/3, in the form of a poorly administered system, remained. W.L. Clay, writing in 1861, foresaw the major panic which was still to come. He noted that the 'real evil, the discharge of criminals unreformed by their past treatment, and without a check on their future conduct, continues unabated' and hoped that 'when the indignant terror of the public is once more aroused, it will not again be squandered on the wrong object' – the unlucky ticket-of-leave.

Even during the panic the reader can discern threads of common sense and moderation amongst the pervading feelings of panic and frustration. Much of the panic writing did have some basis of truth as the system was not working well and there was some evidence of an increase in offences. Some writers, aware of the dangers of the panic itself, appealed for a calmer approach in order that the problem might be solved rationally. Joseph Kingsmill, the Chaplain of Pentonville Prison, wrote that, 'contrary to general opinion, it is certain that the great majority of criminal prisoners in England do not return after release to a course of crime'. Kingsmill also remarked that many of the garotters were probably not ticket-of-leave men but that the increase in crime was a result of the cessation of the Crimean War and the consequent discharge of thousands of troops, 'at no time remarkable for habits of steady industry and now less fit than ever in the arts of peace'.[23] It is remarkable that in the immediate post-Napoleonic war period the discharged soldiery were commonly cited as the cause of the increase in crime but in 1856 very few writers mention it as a probable causal factor.

At the height of the panic the *Daily News* had been willing to attack the address of Baron Alderson to the Liverpool Grand Jury as 'scarcely worthy of the deserved reputation of that eminent judge'. The judge was faced with a calendar that contained 11 tickets-of-leave men out of 108 prisoners and several cases of garotting and he had put these two factors together and launched into a wholesale abuse of the system of conditional discharge, using the current popular arguments which mirrored 'an indignation too hasty for reflection, and a panic too abject for argument'.[24] The newspaper accused Alderson of a fallacy and an oversight. The fallacy was that the end of transportation had resulted from humanitarian prejudice rather than necessity. The oversight was the failure to distinguish between the system of conditional discharge authorised by the 1853 Act and the ticket-of-leave system worked out and operated by the Home Office.

III

The panic of 1856 had led to the Penal Servitude Act of 1857 and the panic of 1862–3 can be cited as the main factor in the passing of the Penal Servitude Act of 1864 and the Prisons Act of 1865. These two pieces of legislation were largely a result of the Royal Commission on Penal Servitude and Transportation and the Select Committee of the House of Lords on discipline in Gaols and Houses of Correction.

As early as August 1862 *The Times* editorial denounced the ticket-of-leave man as the source of street robberies and noted the very lenient sentences handed out by magistrates. *The Times* urged that 'an end must be put to the present mode of granting tickets-of-leave'.[25] *The Times*'s editors came to three conclusions. First, sentences were too short, secondly, the stay in prison was too pleasant and paupers and soldiers were less well-treated than convicts and thirdly there was a lack of police surveillance of released convicts.[26] These sentiments were largely borne out by the findings of the Royal Commission of 1863. Public pressure was such that an inquiry was inevitable and in December 1862, *The Times* wrote that 'the criminal classes never made a greater mistake than when they took to garotting'. The garotters had shown themselves to be enemies of the human race and their acts had to be suppressed 'before society can take time to consider how far an imperfect social condition is responsible for their perversity'. Penal discipline was no longer to be primarily aimed at reforming criminals and this change of opinion had resulted from the revival of 'the whole-some indignation which first gave rise to penal laws' for this 'visible, inexcusable form of crime' had created a general belief that 'right and wrong are, after all, essentially distinct'.[27] The moderate, liberal *Daily News* echoed the sentiments of *The Times*, arguing that it was to save a community from lawlessness that public opinion was demanding a revision in a law which turned convicts loose without supervision and made judges' sentences a fiction.[28]

In December 1862 George Grey announced the setting up of a Royal Commission on Penal Servitude and Transportation and *The Times* explained drily that the ticket-of-leave man, 'took to burglary, to robbery and at length to garotting, but, as that was trying the public patience a little too far, we are once more reviewing our Penal System'.[29]

The Commission's reporting in June 1863 found that the feeling of public outrage was not without justification for they did not 'doubt, that as the law now stands, and has been administered, there has been sufficient cause for the feeling that has arisen'.[30] The evidence received showed that 'the recent increase of offences is at least partly attributable to defects in the systems of punishment now in force'. Much to the reformers' relief the Commission reported that 'the want of sufficient efficacy in the present system of punishment does not seem to arise from any error in its principles' but that the fault lay mainly with the diminished length of sentences and 'in a minor degree, to defects in the discipline to which they are subject'. They found no proper system of supervision of released ticket-of-leave men and no effort made to place them in gainful employment at the time of their release.

The Report recommended longer sentences. They found that sentences had diminished by over 60 per cent, for similar crimes, since the period 1838–42. This was not entirely as a result of legislation, although the Penal Servitude Act of 1857 had made provision for sentences of only three years and the Criminal Law Consolidation Act of 1861 diminished the previous severity of many punishments. It is interesting that the Report should observe:

...the late increase in crime coincides in point of time with the discharge of convicts who were first sentenced for short terms, under the Act of 1857, and is probably attributable in some degree to their release from custody.

The Penal Servitude Act of 1864, which enacted most of the Royal Commission's recommendations, abolished three- and four-year terms of penal servitude and made five years the minimum.

The Report found that the conditions of the licence had not been strictly enforced by the authorities and that the general practice had been to revoke the ticket of leave only on a new conviction. Stricter supervision and enforcement of the existing system was recommended, particularly that re-convicted prisoners should receive severer punishment and not be able to gain remission as a first timer. Although this alteration of remission was provided for by an Act of 1861, it was rarely enforced. The recognition of prisoners as re-convicted was aided five years later by the Habitual Criminals Act of 1869 which provided for the registration of all persons convicted and extended police supervision to minor offenders. The Prevention of Crimes Act of 1871 rendered photographic record of the prisoner compulsory. The Penal Servitude Act of 1864 obliged ticket-of-leave holders to report themselves, not only on discharge, but periodically 'ever after'. The Habitual Criminals Act of 1869 empowered the courts to impose perpetual police supervision on a second conviction. Both these perpetual periods were limited to a maximum of seven years by the Prevention of Crimes Act of 1871.

The Commission reported a need for stricter discipline within prisons. They recommended that the penalty for violence at public works should be increased from two dozen lashes with a light cat to four dozen lashes with a severe cat. The prisoners' diet, they felt, should remain as it was. They found that prisoners' labour was well performed and recommended quarrying and dressing stone as an ideal occupation as it was productive and allowed no communication with free labourers.

They urged the division of prisoners into classes so that violent and dangerous criminals who may need to be subjected to severe coercion were separate from the others. The Commission was in favour of some form of mark system by which the prisoner could achieve higher status (and so, greater gratuities) within the prison but the recommendations did not go as far as the Irish system where the convict had actually to earn his release.

The result of the Report and the Act was a more efficient, better supervised and uniform prison system. For the criminal, the result was longer sentences and in a tougher prison regime. The Report only related to the convict prisons of HM Government. At the same time a Select Commitee of the House of Lords investigated discipline in gaols and houses of correction. Earl Carnavon, announcing the formation of the Select Committee spoke of the awareness of their lordships 'that during a very recent period there was such insecurity in the streets of London that it was dangerous to walk about after nightfall'. The Earl of Dudley said that the whole country believed that the state of crime depended on the manner in which the law was administered.[31] Earl Stanhope had spoken a week earlier of 'the numerous acts of violence' committed since the last session of Parliament and 'how general was the feeling of alarm caused by these outrages'. He believed that there was a general conviction that the system of tickets of leave had not worked well.[32] The report came down hard on the criminal, but eventually led to a more efficient and unified system.

The Select Committee of the House of Lords reported [33] in July 1863 and found the large numbers of re-committals showed 'the inefficiency of the present system of administering the law in ordinary prisons'. The Committee found wide differences in construction of prisons, labour, diet and general discipline leading to an 'inequality, uncertainty and inefficiency of punishment, productive of the most prejudicial results'. The Committee recommended the establishment of uniformity in labour, diet and treatment. To this end they advised that the Treasury should withhold allowance from any gaols where the Secretary of State had issued a code of rules but their acceptance and use was at the discretion of the local authority.

The Report agreed with many of the principles of the liberal prison reformers but found, in practice, that gaol was not always hard enough. They accepted that industrial occupation was beneficial to the prisoner, but felt that the largest part of the labour should be strictly penal. On the 'possible reformation of offenders' in general the Committee thought it 'a necessary part of a sound penal system', but believed that in the interests of both society and the criminal whatever methods of reformation were employed they 'should always be accompanied by due and effective punishment'. In fact the Committee felt 'compelled to admit that the reformation of an individual character by any known process of prison discipline is frequently doubtful'. However, they did believe that prisoners were, 'within certain limits', open to the influences of encouragement and reward and therefore urged the establishment of a system of gradations in every prison rising from the penal and disciplinary labour of the treadwheel, crank or shot-drill, into the higher and less irksome stages of industrial occupation and prison employment. They felt that the Mark System was beneficial for long-term prisoners only and then only to accelerate a prisoner's promotion to a grade 'within certain moderate limits'.

One of the major changes brought about by the Committee was the change in prison construction. They found that association, or a mixed system of association and separation, prevailed but urged legislation to promote the separate system at first by modification of existing gaols and gradually by construction of new gaols. They believed that 'the separate system must now be accepted as the foundation of prison discipline'.

The resulting Prisons Act 1865 (28 and 29 Vict. c. 126) created a harsh regime and took away many of the powers of local authorities.

Prisoners were to be prevented from communicating and kept in separate cells. Hard labour on the treadwheel, shot-drill, crank and capstan and the use of chains and irons were authorised. The Act, according to Philip Collins, reflected a general return to the view that 'prisons should deter through severity instead of making futile attempts to alter prisoners' characters'.[34] The Act of 1865 was strengthened and more rigidly enforced by the Prisons Act 1877 (40 and 41 Vict. c. 121) which placed all borough and county gaols under the control of the Secretary of State, aided by five prison commissioners. Under these commissioners the English prison system became a 'massive machine for the promotion of misery'.[35]

The garotting outbreak of 1862–3 had been brought to the public notice by the press and under pressure from the press and through the medium of the press the public had clamoured for legislation. The legislation on prisons was unimaginative and heavy-handed and created a system from which:

> Prisoners came out into the world numbed and stupid, sometimes insane, often unemployable, nearly always bitter and resentful, with an average (at least for the three years preceding 1878) of seven pence in their pockets, ready to commit more crimes, undeterred and unreformed.[36]

Under the influence of a press-inspired panic, retrograde legislation had been pushed through concerning penal discipline. Although the need for some form of legislation was evident, the specific legislation concerning robbery with violence was unnecessary and an indictment of the parliament that passed it.

IV

At the time that the Garotting Act was debated, as the Security from Violence Bill, Parliament was aware of the trap into which it was being pushed by public opinion represented by the press. Mr Hadfield, member for Sheffield, proposed that the Bill be postponed until the findings of the Royal Commission on Transportation were made known as he 'deprecated all such hasty and ill-considered legislation'.[37] Sir George Grey informed the House that the government had no objection to the introduction of Mr Adderly's Bill but pointed out that the criminal law had been revised and consolidated only two years previously and he reminded the House that on the recommendation of the Select Committee which had carried out the revision, Parliament had agreed, with a few exceptions, to abolish flogging.[38]

Whipping had been used as a form of punishment since the earliest times and when the death penalty prevailed under common law for felonies, whipping was usual for misdemeanours, normally at the cart's tail, or, later, at a public whipping post.[39] Throughout the nineteenth century the trend was to stop whipping as a punishment for adults. In 1820 the whipping of females was abolished by Act 1 Geo. IV c.57. By the Vagrancy Act 1824 justices' power to authorise the public whipping of vagrants was limited to second and subsequent offences only. By 1861 Parliament had adopted the two principles that no one should be whipped twice for the same offence and that public whippings should be discontinued. However, it was not long before a breach was made in these general principles. This breach was the Security from Violence Act which allowed for 'Once, twice or thrice whipping'. The Act prescribed a maximum of 25 strokes for under 16 year-olds and 50 for those over 16 years. For adults a heavy birch was used, 48 inches long with a handle 22 inches long weighing 12 ounces with a spray at the centre of 7 inches circumference. The cat-o'nine-tails was composed of nine lengths of fine whipcord, whipped at the ends to prevent fraying, and attached to a short handle.

The two main arguments against the Bill which came out in the parliamentary debate were first, that the punishment was degrading and that therefore juries would be disinclined to convict and secondly, that there was no real cause for the panic and therefore no cause for the legislation.

Adderly argued that George Grey's contention that juries would not convict was a fallacy as 'the Home Secretary had entirely mistaken the feeling of the public'. Adderly believed that the universal feeling was that punishments were too weak and uncertain and that 'a greater variety of punishments must be devised to meet new and increasing forms of outrage'.[40] He believed that the country was in favour of the death penalty for a second conviction for garotting. At the second reading of the Bill in the House of Lords, the Earl of Carnavon argued that to say that flogging was degrading, 'gives the class of which garotters are usually composed credit for motives and feelings which they neither possess nor comprehend'.[41]

The major point was raised at the second reading of the Bill in the Commons by Clay, who stated that the Bill was advocated upon the theory that it was necessitated by an exceptional state of crime and that before he voted he would have to be satisfied that such an exceptional state of crime really existed otherwise MPs would be 'liable to the imputation of legislating under an unreasonable state of panic'. Clay stated that he believed 'that the idea of an extraordinary prevalence of the crime of garotting was wholly and entirely untrue'. Having spoken to magistrates and police, 'he thought there was an immense amount of exaggerated fear abroad with respect to this crime'.[42]

Sir George Grey, when Home Secretary, agreed with Clay 'that there had been great exaggerations in many cases alleged to have occurred'. He explained his interpretation of the situation as an above-average number of robberies with violence in London which led to a fashion in such crimes. He believed the publicity given to the attack on Pilkington 'had actually prompted the commission of similar outrages'. The number of plainclothes police had been increased and many such criminals had been apprehended and convicted at the Central Criminal Court. So, asked Grey, 'Where was the necessity for Parliament to alter the law?' and he declared that the House was about to enact 'panic legislation after the panic had subsided'.[43]

Logic was not to prevail and the sentiments which Colonel North represented led to the Royal Assent being given to the Bill on 13 July 1863 (26 and 27 Vict. c. 44). In the committee stage North professed that he could not understand the sympathy manifested for the delicate feelings of a garotter, and thought nothing so likely to put a stop to the offence as a good, sound flogging. It was said the crime was on the decrease but, according to North, the fact was that these London performers were 'starting it in the provinces'.[44]

In retrospect it was generally agreed that the Security from Violence Act was an unnecessary and ineffective measure. The 1938 Report on Corporal Punishment noted that the number of persons convicted at the Central Criminal Court of robbery with violence increased in 1865 and 1866. Sir George Grey, whilst introducing the Penal Servitude Bill in February 1864 stated that robbery with violence cases in the metropolis had numbered 82 in the last six months of 1862 compared to only 26 in the same period for 1863. However, he was of the opinion that this was not a result of the Security from Violence Act which had been little used but 'through the vigilance and activity of the police'.[45] Writing in 1888, James Greenwood commented that 'somehow or other the stinging thongs seemed to be wielded with but little effect'.[46] T.B. Lloyd-Baker, writing in 1867, regarded the Act as wholly unnecessary as he believed that garotting had been stopped because the police quietly put pressure on ticket-of-leave men so that the public and the press could turn to other matters, 'the former happy to forget its fears, the latter having some newer excitement to turn to – and the garotte fever was at an end'.[47]

The garotte outbreak and its associated panic had led to an

unnecessary and ineffective piece of legislation which was fragmentary and reactionary. It was a piece of legislation of which any parliamentarian could be justifiably ashamed.

V

The Tithebarn Street murder and the disproportionate press coverage it received formed the basis for a public discussion on brutality. *The Times* was later to criticise the slum-life in Liverpool and the *Spectator* was to level criticism at the inaction of the town council but first the public had to be alarmed into taking an interest.

The *Spectator* first printed the story on 8 August 1874 and although admitting that the atrocity, was 'not actually the most sickening that has occurred', stated that it was 'undoubtedly the one which ought most to alarm society, and to stir up magistrates, the public, and we must add, the Judges, to secure a more rigid enforcement of the law'.[48] The editor believed the problem 'had been left far too long unrestrained by magistrates who seem to think a murderous assault a trivial crime, if only the victim, however mutilated, manages to keep alive'. The *Spectator* claimed that 'for months past' the press and the 'decent portion of the public' (whom the *Spectator* clearly claimed to represent) had been pressing for harsher sentences for those convicted of brutal assaults. This view was echoed by the *Liverpool Town Crier* (12 August 1874) which stated that, 'the people can find no satisfaction in the sentencing of a man who kicks a fellow man almost lifeless to a short imprisonment'.

The Times decided to print the story on 11 August and gave their view that this motiveless murder was the culmination of a growing habit of brutality and that 'wherever it is prevalent, civilisation must of necessity come to an end'. In addition to this general warning that civilisation (in the context of *The Times* this was synonymous with middle-class life) would end if brutal crimes increased, it was also brought home in a dramatic personal warning to readers that, for the brutal attacker, 'his reason for murder is your existence, his place the public street, his opportunity the fact that you are passing and have a head to be smashed, ribs to be pounded, a life to be kicked out of you'.

Prior to the Tithebarn Street murder, violence had been brought to Parliament's attention owing to the prevalence of wife-beating. Colonel Egerton Leigh had asked Assheton Cross, the Home Secretary, on 24 July 1874, whether a measure for the additional protection of women and children from the violence of men would be introduced in the next session. The Home Secretary replied that the matter was under the consideration of the government to see whether a legislative measure was required.[49] With mounting pressure from the press following the Tithebarn Street murder, Cross issued a circular to Her Majesty's Judges, the Chairmen of Quarter Sessions, Recorders, Stipendiary Magistrates, Magistrates of Metropolitan Police Courts and Sheriffs of Scotland on 15 October 1874 concerning all forms of brutal assault. The circular was to enable the Home Office to consider 'measures to be adopted for the more effective repression of the crimes of violence, now unhappily so common among certain classes of the population'.[50]

The Times was 'glad to see the attention of the Home Secretary had been attracted to the frequent occurrence of crimes of brutal violence'.[51] The newspaper then proceeded to judge the Home Secretary by its own unstatistical standards, writing that 'we need not ask, nor, we observe, does the Home Office ask ... whether these crimes have been on the increase. It is enough to know that they are very common'. In fact the Home Office did call for statistics on the number of brutal assaults from the chief constables of each county. For the years 1870 to 1874 the chief constables were required to supply annual figures detailing brutal assaults on women and children (summary and indictable) and brutal assaults on men (summary and indictable).

The first point for discussion in the press was whether flogging should be introduced for brutal assault. *The Times* took its usual stance. In its opinion, flogging had put a stop to garotting and so, 'flogging has almost put down the one offence, and it would just as easily put down the other too'. *The Times* was of the opinion that any law was useless that failed to 'terrify those who break it', and that 'there can, we imagine, be little doubt felt as to the preventive efficacy of flogging'. It is little wonder that the *Daily Post* remarked that *The Times* wrote on this subject, 'with a strangely bitter animus'.[52] However, other organs of the press supported the view of *The Times*. *The Porcupine* feared that the present generation of roughs was beyond redemption by educational and moral agencies and that 'the only chance of repression seems to be to strike terror into their ranks by prompt and severe punishment'.[53] The *Liverpool Town Crier* believed that the examples set by the sentences of the courts were to no avail and 'what is wanted is known as the "cat"'.[54] Only the *Spectator* took a more enlightened line. Their editorials did not argue in favour of flogging but in favour of the certainty of the punishment. The *Daily Post* found this stance difficult to contend with. 'It would be difficult to say', they wrote, 'whether the London accuser, or the local official defenders of Liverpool in the matter of street violence, talk more foolishly'.[55] This was partly a reaction to *The Times* which had by now altered its tack and taken to attacking Liverpool and its local institutions as being the cause of brutality which it now saw as a specifically Liverpudlian problem. The *Spectator* replied that, the *Liverpool Daily Post* does not quite understand our position with respect to the repression of crimes',[56] and repeated that certainty of punishment is the most important condition for the effective repression of crime. They also believed that juries would not convict if flogging was the punishment.

By early 1875 the Home Secretary was beginning to receive replies to his circular and it was the *Spectator* which reported, without adverse comment, that the ex-Home Secretary, Lord Aberdare, had stated that flogging for brutal assaults had been persistently tried before and had failed, and that garotting had been stopped, if it had been stopped, by espionage and not by whipping. *Punch* found little sympathy with Aberdare's views. Commenting in one of his earlier speeches at Brighton it expressed the view that Aberdare found no solace from the fact that a cruel ruffian 'had been scourged to the effect of making him howl some time for mercy' and adjudged that, 'to this extent Lord Aberdare is evidently deficient in the heart that can feel for another'.[57]

Towards the spring of 1875 this cry for vengeful flogging was muted in the press. Editors were aware that the replies to the Home Secretary's circular had been largely in favour of flogging and felt that legislation was forthcoming. As early as December 1874, Mr Justice Mellor, addressing the Grand Jury of Liverpool, noted that, 'a great outcry has taken place for more legislation' and that although, 'it is always dangerous to legislate in haste; but, at the same time, I think the steps which have been taken to ascertain the general feeling of all who have to administer justice may lead us to the expectation that some further legislation is in prospect'.[58]

It seemed that the emotional outcry had succeeded. Two of the three murderers had been hanged and it seemed that legislation would follow. The Liverpool press was still taking political sides over the issue of the town council's inefficiency. The national press now turned to other issues or hypocritically offered advice to the legislators on the dangers of legislating in haste. The best examples of this hypocrisy came from *The Times* which in March 1875 argued that although 'there is so much to be said in favour of inflicting corporal chastisement on brutal offenders', it warned that with the present state of public feeling 'there is some danger that too much will be done rather than too little and we may run the risk of brutalising ourselves in the very vehemence of our efforts to restrain the savagery of our neighbours'.[59] One notes that no mention was made that the state of public feeling was in part aroused by *The Times*'s own articles. In the same editorial *The Times* suddenly adopted the arguments of the *Spectator* and contended that, 'On a review of the whole case we should incline to be well satisfied if we were assured that Mr Cross's Bill would provide that the existing penalties of the law should be put more regularly into force'.

On 7 May 1875, Cross introduced a Bill 'for the further security of the persons of Her Majesty's subjects from violence'. Cross said that it was evident that further provision was necessary for dealing with cases of brutal violence and proposed to extend the power given to magistrates with regard to binding over persons guilty of aggravated assaults to keep the peace. It was also proposed to do something about flogging by giving the power to impose a sentence of flogging to the Courts of Oyer and Terminer in cases of assault with intent to commit grievous bodily harm, and in cases of aggravated assaults on women and children, but the number of lashes was to be reduced from 50 to 25.[60]

However, Parliament had learned by its mistakes, and especially from the panic legislation of the Security from Violence Act of 1863, that flogging was no longer an acceptable solution, if solution it ever was. Sir Wilfred Lawson warned Cross that he 'must be prepared to expect a determined opposition to that part of the Bill which proposed to inflict the torture of flogging'.[61] The opposition was certainly determined and as Cross realised, commanded a majority of support. The Bill was withdrawn on 26 July 1875.

VI

By the 1870s with the wealth of social legislation that was planned, Parliament was beginning to face a problem which is even more pronounced in present times – lack of time. It may be assumed that it had learned from its piecemeal, ineffective and retrograde legislation resulting from the panics of the 1850s and 1860s and perhaps no longer desired to respond so hastily to a public opinion which having been whipped to a frenzy by the agency of the press tended to subside quickly, quite often before the legislation had been enacted. At the same time the shortage of parliamentary time prevented the government from reacting with legislation in response to such panics. Such an institutionalised regulator should be seen as beneficial to the state of society for laws, hastily enacted and however inefficient, remain on the statute book for many decades and affect society long after the panic has subsided. The Security from Violence Act remained on the statute books until the Criminal Justice Act of 1948 after which flogging was limited to punishment for violence to prison officers, for mutiny and for inciting mutiny by prisoners. As a result of a doubtfully-based, press-inspired panic, this statute had survived for eighty-five years and during that time never proved effective. As Hibbert notes, the effect of ending flogging as a punishment for robbery with violence in 1948 was noticeable – for the three years before 1948 there had been an average of 874 robberies with violence per annum. In the three years after, the average fell to 768.[62]

Similarly the harsh and hasty penal legislation of the 1850s and 1860s remained until the Prisons Act 1898 (61 and 62 Vict. c.41) introduced a more enlightened, and certainly no less effective administration of the British prison system. In the meantime, hundreds of thousands of prisoners had lived in miserable conditions in prisons and, if convicted of robbery with violence, had received countless lashings with the cat or beatings with the birch, because for a few months in the 1850s and 1860s the press had decided to manufacture news and create a moral panic which demanded action in the form of legislation.

Notes

1. Sir J.F. Stephen, *A Digest of the Criminal Law* (1887), XXI.
2. G.R. Scott, *The History of Corporal Punishment* (1948), xxiii.
3. H. Jones, *Crime in a Changing Society* (1965), ii.
4. W.L. Clay, *The Prison Chaplain* (1861).
5. R. and F. Davenport-Hill *A Memoir of Matthew Davenport-Hill* (1878).
6. *Hansard*, 3rd series, Vol. CXXVI, 665, 28 April 1853.
7. Ibid., 666–679, 28 April 1853.
8. *Hansard*, 3rd Series, Vol. 127, 1–78, 10 May 1853.
9. *The Times*, 10 November 1856.
10. Letter from F.W.L., *The Times*, 9 December 1856.
11. Letter from George S. Jenkinson, *The Times*, 18 October 1855.
12. Letter from Joshua Jebb, *The Times*, 18 October 1855.
13. Letter from Joshua Jebb, *The Times*, 28 December 1855.
14. *Morning Chronicle*, 16 September 1856.
15. *Daily News*, 10 September 1856.
16. *Daily News*, 12 September 1856.
17. *Morning Chronicle*, 15 December 1856.
18. *Blackwood's Edinburgh Mgazine*, Vol. 81, February 1857, 173–188.
19. *Morning Chronicle*, 15 December 1856.
20. *Morning Chronicle*, 18 December 1856.
21. Report of Select Committee on Transportation, *P.P. (1856)*, c.244 XVII q.79.
22. T.B. Lloyd-Baker, *War Against Crime*, (1889) 15.
23. Letter from Joseph Kingsmill, *The Times*, 3 January 1857.
24. *Daily News*, 10 December 1856.

25. *The Times*, 15 August 1862.
26. *The Times*, 28 August 1862.
27. *The Times*, 30 December 1862.
28. *Daily News*, 1 December 1862.
29. *The Times*, 16 February 1863.
30. Report of the Royal Commission on Penal Servitude and Transportation, *P.P. (1863)* c.3190, Vol. XXI.
31. *Hansard*, 19 February 1863, 477 and 492.
32. *Hansard*, 10 February 1863, 215–6.
33. Report of the Select Committee of the House of Lords on the Present State of Discipline in Gaols and Houses of Correction, *P.P. (1863)* c.499, Vol.IX.
34. P. Collins, *Dickens and Crime* (1962), 19.
35. D.L. Howard, *English Prisons* (1960), 103.
36. C. Hibbert, The *Roots of Evil* (1963), 188.
37. *Hansard*, 11 March 1863, 1306.
38. *Hansard*, 24 February 1863, 787.
39. Much of the following information is taken from the Report of the Departmental Committee on Corporal Punishment, *P.P. (1938)*, ix.
40. *Hansard*, 11 March 1863, 1304.
41. *Hansard*, 9 June 1863, 555.
42. *Hansard*, 11 March 1863, 1309.
43. *Hansard*, 11 March 1863, 1310.
44. *Hansard*, 6 May 1863, 1278.
45. *Hansard*, 18 February 1864, 724–5.
46. J. Greenwood, *The Policeman's Lantern: Strange Stories of London Life* (1881) 31.
47. T.B. Lloyd-Baker, op.cit., 24.
48. *Spectator*, 8 August 1874.
49. *Hansard*, Vol, 221, 24 July 1874, 624.
50. *P.P. (1875)*, Vol. LXI, c. 1138.
51. *The Times*, 24 October 1874.
52. *Daily Post*, 12 January 1875.
53. *The Porcupine*, 19 December 1874.
54. *Liverpool Town Crier*, 23 December 1874.
55. *Daily Post*, 12 January 1875.
56. *Spectator*, 16 January 1875.
57. *Punch*, 23 October 1875.
58. *Liverpool Mail*, 12 December 1874.
59. *The Times*, 11 January 1875.
60. *Hansard*, 7 May 1875, 209.
61. *Hansard*, 7 May 1875, 209.
62. Hibbert, op.cit., 445.

8. The Effect of the Panics on the Courts

I

Cohen's model of folk devils forecasts a pyramidal conception of blame whereby, at first, the press and public would automatically blame the police. If the police appeared to be acting in an acceptable way the next level where blame could be apportioned would be in the action in the courts. If these courts were found blameless then the Home Secretary, the prison system and the legislature warranted investigation. Somebody or something had to be at fault. In the incidents of reported street violence in the nineteenth century the police, on the whole, seemed to have escaped blame, as did the courts. If anything, the judiciary acquired the mantle of folk heroes as the judges and magistrates were willing to hand out heavy sentences and make examples of certain poor individuals to rid the country of folk devils.

Did the press-engendered panics really affect the sober arbiters of the law in the United Kingdom? In order to attempt to answer the question one must first look at who these arbiters of the law were; then one must attempt to weigh up the possibilities of their being influenced by the press; and finally one must discover if their sentencing policies changed during such panics.

II

The basis of the English judicial system was the institution of the justices of the peace or magistrates who had had the power of summary jurisdiction over relatively minor crimes since their establishment in 1363. Prior to 1848 this power was exercised singly. The Summary Jurisdiction Act of that year consolidated the provisions for holding Petty Sessions and required JPs to sit in pairs. More serious crimes were heard by superior courts which had unlimited jurisdiction. These were

Quarter Sessions, presided over by judges. Such judges were appointed by the Crown with the commission of oyer and terminer (to hear and determine). Prior to 1875 there were two short terms of Michaelmas and Easter when judges of the various courts sat individually or together (in banc) in London. After these terms they went on one of six circuits to hear cases on assize. This meant that the courts did not sit for five months of the year but then sat for three months at a stretch. The Judicature Act 1875 allowed for Assizes to be held at the same time as sittings in London; it gave some towns three assizes instead of two; it increased the number of circuits from six to seven and to emphasise the unity of the Supreme Court it allowed for all judges to be sent on assize, even those of the Chancery Division. This system led to arrears of business in London and was abandoned in 1884. In 1877, Cross, the Home Secretary, abolished some assize towns but introduced a fourth assize in September or October each year in selected towns.[1] Both Liverpool and Manchester benefited from these arrangements. Until the Court of Criminal Appeal was set up in 1907 there was no means by which judicial decisions could be reversed except by the intervention of the Home Secretary exercising the royal prerogative of mercy, whereas following the Judicature Act 1873 cases in Petty and Quarter Sessions could be heard on appeal before the Queen's Bench Division of the High Court of Justice. Queen's (or King's) Bench, Common Pleas and Exchequer originally had clearly defined and separate jurisdictions but by 1750 their jurisdictions were identical. From the judges of these three central courts the itinerant Commissioners of Assize were drawn.

The justices of the peace held wide discretionary powers over many areas of local government. To administer county and judicial affairs the magistrates met at the Quarter Sessions four times each year. These gatherings were presided over by the Lord Lieutenant of the county who was the military commander, chief magistrate and leading landed magnate. The JPs were responsible for setting the price of bread, the rates for common carriers and the wages and regulating the behaviour of servants and workmen. They were also responsible for: licensing physicians, bankers, actors and alehouses; controlling the activities of church wardens and vagrants; collecting excise and stamp duties; ordering the construction of prisons, bridges and asylums; administering criminal proceedings; superintending roads, public buildings and charitable institutions; authorising the use of boats on Sundays; and enlisting constables to restore order in times of civil unrest.[2]

Between Quarter Sessions magistrates conducted fortnightly or monthly Petty Sessions in their home districts. There was inconsistency in the justice administered by the JPs and magistrates could be ruthless in their efforts to stamp out certain forms of behaviour. Jerome K. Jerome, the literary observer of life, remarked in 1900 that whereas in Germany misdemeanour had its fixed price, in England one had sleepless nights not knowing whether one would be let off with a caution, fined forty shillings, or 'catching the magistrate in an unhappy moment for yourself get seven days'.[3] The magistracy were under no obligation to submit their policies to the Home Secretary or any other authority and their powers of discretion were so great as to render it impossible to determine whether they had exceeded their powers. Throughout the 1840s poaching and arson were treated harshly although Jones reports that in Merthyr Tydfil, from 1846, it was stealing from the person which was punished more severely than any other crime. In the slum area of 'China', where the number of assaults was high, Superintendent Wren and Constable Thomas Vigors carried out a private war. Their work was supported by magistrates like H.A. Bruce and T.W. Hill, thereby winning 'the admiration of middle-class residents and the press'.[4]

Throughout the century the criminal proceedings presided over by these untrained, lay magistrates, increased. In 1857 justices in Quarter Sessions dealt with four times the number of indictable offences dealt with by judges on assize and justices in Petty Sessions dealt with twenty times more cases than all the other criminal courts. In 1862 Petty Sessions sent six times more people to prison than the Quarter Sessions and Assizes combined.[5]

J.P. Dunbabin notes that the JPs were 'a largely self co-opting group of notables'.[6] They were appointed by the Crown, having been nominated by the Lord Lieutenant (who was appointed by the Lord Chancellor). In 1835 the Municipal Corporations Act stripped the borough magistrates of all but their judicial duties, allowing the elected municipal councils to select lay magistrates, stipendiary (i.e. paid) magistrates and Recorders who were part-time judges appointed from the practising bar. It was the 1835 Act which allowed a greater number of the middle classes to enter the borough magistracy. In the other administrative districts the social composition of the magistracy remained landed for a considerable period. An Act of 1732 made ownership of an estate with a minimum annual income of £100 the minimum requirement for the appointment of a magistrate. This qualification, the unsalaried status and the process of co-option effectively excluded all but the landed gentry. In 1875 an attempt to have the £100 qualification removed was defeated. From mid-century the County Magistracy did begin to lower its class barriers in order to admit the upper middle classes to the bench as is demonstrated by Zangerl's research. The institution of the Justices of the Peace was not geared to urban growth and the problems which it created. It was an institution of the traditional paternalistic age which could not cope with urbanisation and industrialisation. The Municipal Corporations Act allowed for a middle-class magistracy representing the new commercial interest to develop in the new municipal boroughs but the rest of the country was left with an anachronistic system which was not suited to the new urban conditions.

III

The city courts before which the cases considered in this study were heard were either Quarter Sessions, presided over largely by stipendiary magistrates or Recorders, or Assizes presided over by judges. Unlike the county justices who would have performed the task as a paternalistic duty handed down from generation to generation, the stipendiary magistrates were part of the growing business of urban politics.

Because of the system of co-option, the rural JPs merely had to impress the other JPs on the bench. The stipendiary magistrate was appointed by an elected municipal corporation and so had to be conscious of his image with the enfranchised. The enfranchised in the new boroughs were precisely the middle class whose attentions the press commanded and so it seems likely that such officers of the court would, if not consciously courting newspaper publicity, be more mindful of avoiding negative publicity than their well-established, amateur, rural counterparts. Such negative publicity was attracted by Mr Hopwood QC, the Recorder of Liverpool in 1886. Following the November Assizes when Mr Justice Day had administered a law of terror, Mr Hopwood was accused of administering a law of leniency when he gave very light sentences for cases of wounding at the Borough Sessions. Nott-Bower, the Chief Constable, later noted that the press comment – 'undoing of the wholesome work of the Judges of Assize', 'intense egotism', 'folly and inconsistency' 'inane comments', 'mockery of justice', etc., – 'seemed hardly excessive'.[7] One does not have to look far through an index of letters to *The Times* to observe that magistrates did write to such newspapers and so must have regarded them as having some influence. Baron Martin had 'no pretension to the arts of advocacy at the Bar, and he was a man of little learning' while Mr Justice Lush had never seen the inside of a Criminal Court until he was appointed a judge. Of Mr Justice Malins it was said that he was characterised by 'not so much ignorance of the law as want of sympathy with law as a system'.[8] If called to the bar they would then attempt to make a living as a special pleader on one of the circuits, arguing commercial cases on behalf of clients. One built up a reputation on circuit and hoped to be appointed a Queen's Counsel, like Baron Weston, who joined the Northern Circuit in 1832, where he found work and became popular, and was appointed a QC in 1843.

From 1825 the Chief Justice of the King's Bench received an annual salary of £10,000 and superior court judges £5,500. From 1832 these salaries were reduced to £8,000 and £5,000 respectively. Pensions varied between £3,500 and £3,750, but were only payable after fifteen years' service as a judge giving every incentive to remain a member of the judiciary despite senility.[9] Such senility was perhaps evident in the remarks and actions of Sir John Day, who handed out the flogging sentences to the High Rip in Liverpool in 1887. He had been appointed as a judge in 1872. He was a firm believer in the lash and the sentences he dealt out for minor offences were extraordinary and 'seemed lost to all sense of proportion'. This was the result of his Roman Catholicism and it was observed that 'the intensity of religious convictions swayed his judicial calmness'. He showed 'a stern-ness and upheld a standard of conduct which belonged to another age'. In 1888, with Smith and Hannen, he was appointed to the Parnell Commission which led to complaints in Parliament as he had made some 'ill-judged remarks about Irishmen' at the Liverpool Assizes a few years earlier. In the House of Commons, 30 July 1888, John Morley MP read the following quotation from a private letter written by Judge Adams, one of the Belfast Commissioners: 'Mr Justice Day is a man of the seventeenth century in his views, a catholic as strong as Torquemada, a tory of the old high-flyer and non-juror type'.[10] Lush had been appointed a Judge of Appeal too late, when the elasticty of his mind had begun to fail. Signs of failure were visible at the last assize which he attended when he had 'an appearance of physical breaking up'. The importance of the fifteen years was shown by Justice Byles who retired in the middle of a term after exactly the required amount of service plus one day.[11]

It may have been the thought of a pension which made Sir Charles Parker Butt remain as judge despite the fact that even as he delivered heavy sentences on the High Rip gang in 1886 his health was 'gravely impaired' by a 'painful malady' and 'in such circumstances a great lawyer must have failed to establish a reputation commensurate with his powers'.[12]

A study of the biographies of Sir William Watson (1798-1860) who presided over the Central Criminal Court in November 1856; Sir George Bramwell (1808-92) who presided over the Central Criminal Court in November 1862; Sir Samuel Martin (1801-83) who presided over the Winter Assize at Manchester in 1865 and Sir Robert Lush (1807–81) who presided over that of the next year; Sir Charles Parker Butt (1830–92) and Sir John Day (1826–1908), reveals that even the successful members of the profession took between eleven and seventeen years to be appointed a Queen's Counsel. They then waited between four and thirteen years to be knighted. In the cases of Watson, Bramwell and Martin the knighthood was the automatic result of being appointed to a Baron of the Court of the Exchequer which court ceased to exist as of 1876. (The Court of the Exchequer sat annually on the day after St Martin' day to decide issues of revenue between subjects and Crown and for the swearing of the Chancellor of the Exchequer to the due application of the secret service money.)

Such men were public figures and would therefore desire to acquire and maintain a favourable public image. Hence Watson was described as a 'judge possessed of a clear head and strong mind', Day was 'an authority on the new methods of pleading and practice', while Bramwell, 'one of the strongest judges that ever sat on the bench', earned the reputation of a formidable antagonist of defence lawyers who entered pleas of insanity. In his first year as a judge in 1851 he had tried a man called Dove who killed his wife whilst allegedly insane. Bramwell had 'stated the law to the jury with so much force, accuracy and lucidity' that Dove was found guilty and hanged.

For the next twenty years he gave short shrift to 'mad doctors' called as witnesses by the defence. Martin, also distinguished by his lucidity and force in presenting points to the jury, acquired a reputation as one who 'did not shrink from imposing heavy sentences when demanded by justice'.[13] That these men were conscious of their public image is demonstrated by the fact that three – Watson, Martin and Butt – contested and eventually won seats as Liberal members of parliament while Bramwell was a member of the Property Defence League. For a judge to be in politics was unremarkable. Indeed, the opposite was the case, for it was remarked that Lush 'had no politics'.[14] Baron Cleasby contested Surrey (twice) and Cambridge University for the Tories. In return for contesting the Cambridge seat unsuccessfully in 1868, Lord Cairns made him a judge although he 'never had much practice at the bar'. Byles was a strong Tory and Thesiger was a political appointee of Lord Beaconsfield who, as Prime Minister, had the power to appoint Lord Justices. If it had not been for his early death at forty-two years, Thesiger would have been destined to be the future Conservative Chancellor.[15] There seems to be evidence that these men were aware that they were public figures and needed to maintain a favourable public image with the enfranchised. The classic example was Chief

Justice Cockburn, Lord Chief Justice Coleridge, of whom it was said that none loved their reputation as he loved his. Cockburn's hold on the public mind was attributed to his reputation of having passed a somewhat stormy youth and he was criticised for 'a weakness for being before the public' to the point that he would prolong inquiries 'raising topics of general interest in which he could be the central figure'.[16] Did they, however, regard the press as being influential and instrumental in maintaining such an image? The evidence seems to imply that they did.

IV

Many aspiring politicians went into journalism as a first career whilst awaiting their entry into public life. Butt was one such. He had acted as a correspondent to *The Times* at Constantinople before being called to the bar in 1854. He unsuccessfully contested Tamworth for the Liberals in 1874 and eventually became the Member for Southampton in 1880 before being knighted in 1884. Bramwell certainly believed in the power of the fourth estate, being an avid writer to the newspapers under the pseudonym 'B' and it was reported that 'his summings-up were as terse, clear, easy to understand, as his letters to the newspapers'.[17] Fairfield's biography of Bramwell contains many clues as to the judge's attitude to the press. Fairfield believed that Bramwell was raised to the post of Baron of the Exchequer partly as a reward for his sitting on the parliamentary commission 1853–61 which led to the Companies Act of 1862, but mainly 'to comply with the general wish of the legal profession (and at the behest of *The Times*)'. Although Fairfield believed English and Scottish judges were singularly unhated and were 'out of range even of newspaper attacks' he later noted that on the morning that Lord Blackburn was raised to the Bench *The Times* asked in a leader 'Who is Mr Blackburn?'.

Bramwell wrote to a brother judge, Baron Channell, on his retirement, that 'What *The Times* said of you is what all think and say', while Sir William Erle wrote to Bramwell that he was comforted to see the actions of a mutual friend were 'duly appreciated by *The Times* and therefore by Her Majesty's public in general'. On 7 January 1856, Sir John Mellor wrote to Bramwell on his appointment as a judge: 'I congratulate you and the profession, but pray do not go and hang people right and left to please *The Times*. See article today ...' It appears to be doubtful as to whether this advice was heeded, for Bramwell 'resented it keenly' and was 'evidently rather angry', if articles appeared criticising his actions while he became 'a terror to the leaders' in the

House of Lords because of his shrewdness, humour, grasp of fact but chiefly because 'he had the run of *The Times*'. 'Thousands of readers' were amused or edified by what Bramwell wrote on the subjects of drink and land nationalisation and his pamphlets were often published in full in *The Times* and *Nineteenth Century*, and when criticised by Joseph Chamberlain in political speeches *The Times* leaders leapt to Bramwell's defence. By the end of his career Bramwell was actually writing leaders for *The Times*. Throughout his career he 'strove vigorously in the House of Lords and in the columns of *The Times* for freedom of contract'.[18] In the biography of his father, Arthur Day wrote that Sir John Day 'never curried favour with the public, the press or the powers that be', although the fact that such a denial was necessary implies that other judges did curry such favour. His son also believed that Day was punished by certain newspapers for his independent attitude and that in revenge they would record his having done things which he specially abominated, such as never being happier than when smoking a long cigar.[19] Despite this independence of the press, Day was aware of its presence. *Punch* greeted his appointment with the quip that 'the next step will be to turn Day into Knight, and may it be very long before the break of Day',[20] and there is a reminiscence of present-day publicity stunts in Day's visiting Armley Gaol in Leeds and doing a full stint on the treadmill, in 1883, which led to a woodcut in the next issue of *Punch*.[21]

Thesiger was the brother of Lord Chelmsford who had been routed by the Zulus at Isandlwana in 1879 and he spent much time writing letters to the newspapers to sustain his brother's reputation until it was restored by the action at Ulundi in 1880. The ability of the press to ruin a man was experienced by Chief Baron Kelly in 1876. Having sat on the Judicial Committee which heard the case of Risdale v. Clifton, Kelly later confided to the Sheriff's chaplain on the North Wales circuit that he had dissented from the judgment of the majority and regarded the judgment as policy, not law. The Sheriff's chaplain wrote to the newspapers adding that Kelly had described the judgment as iniquitous. He was upbraided by Lord Cairns, the Lord Chancellor, and as a result never received a peerage. As he refused to retire without a peerage, he never retired, but became a 'veteran who lagged too late upon the stage'.[22] For some judges, a good reputation with the press was unnecessary as long as harmful publicity was avoided. For example, Justice Hatherley owed his success to his connection with the City and the fact that his father was an ex-Sheriff of London. Baron Martin married the daughter of Chief Baron Pollock who made no attempt to hide his partiality in cases where his son-in-law appeared. On one occasion. Thesiger, as counsel for the defence, complained in court that with Martin prosecuting before Pollock 'it was impossible for counsel to do his duty'.[23] For most, however, reputations were important.

These were public men with ambition and reputations to build and safeguard, who were very clear as to the power of the serious press in evolving and enhancing such reputations. Whether they reacted in their punishment policy to press panics is the subject of the next section.

V

In order to ascertain the responses of the judiciary to the outbreaks of reporting and comment in the press the punishments for street violence offences in Middlesex, Liverpool and Manchester for the forty-year period were analysed using the following scale:

Punishment		Units
Death		10
Transportation	7 – 10 years	5
	11 years – life	7
Penal Servitude	0 – 3 years	5
	4 – 7 years	6
	10 – 20 years	10
Imprisonment	0 – 6 months	1
	6 months – 1 year	2
	1 – 2 years	3
	2 – 3 years	4
	3 – 4 years	5
Flogging		1
Other (fines, bound over)		½

Such units are not totally arbitrary. When transportation ceased the sentence of seven years transportation was replaced by three years penal servitude and so the equal unit figure of five has some justification. It is arguable whether twenty years penal servitude was equal to a death sentence as the equal unit figure of ten implies, but the use of a unit figure does aid in the comparison of different levels of punishment of varying kinds. Hence a unit figure of five implies that the average person appearing before the court (whether found guilty or not) for a street violence offence received a sentence equal in severity to three or four years imprisonment or up to three years penal servitude.

Throughout 1851 *The Times* had increased its reporting of garottings in London and published a series of letters on the subject in July of that year. The unit figure for punishment rises steeply to 6.5 in September and 6.2 in December in the Middlesex figures compared to an average for the preceding twenty months of 2.5. These figures were not to be reached again until the scare of 1856, except for the exceptional figures of 6.6 in August 1852 and 7.0 in December 1854. The August 1852 figure was a result of only five persons appearing before the court charged with street violence offences of which three were given sentences in excess of 10 years' penal servitude. The December 1854 figure was caused by there being only one case of street violence for which the defendant was transported for life. In September 1856 the contrast was more startling. The unit figure was 7.5 compared to an average of the preceding twenty months of 1.9. In the 1850s the unit figure only rose above 6.0 (except for the freak August 1852 and December 1854) without prior publicity in December 1857, and even this may have been a partial result of the previous year's pressure, with the public fearing a repetition of the previous winter's 'garotting epidemic'. Outside London punishments seemed to remain uniform except for the Lancashire Assizes of 1854 which produced three very high figures (6.6., 6.1., 5.4.) compared to those of the Assizes of the previous four years. There is no obvious explanation for this phenomenon. The publicity of 1862 led to a figure of 6.3 for the November Sessions, compared to an average since the beginning of the decade of 1.2. This figure was not surpassed again during the decade except for November 1866 which was a depression year of working-class agitation when the courts were on their guard and determined to give deterrent sentences. The publicity surrounding the London roughs of June 1867 managed to produce the highest figure for that particular year, although the nature of the offences kept it to an otherwise unremarkable 3.5.

The most noticeable outcome of the Trafalgar Square riot and its aftermath in February 1886 is the high number of acquittals and small numbers appearing before the courts, both probably resulting from the disorganisation of the police on the particular days in question. In February 1886 only 17 of the 74 cases tried were for street violence and of these five were acquitted. In March 1886, the same number of cases produced six street violence cases of which five were acquitted.

The Manchester garotters produced the highest figure of the decade (6.0) at the Manchester Assizes in 1866. The other figure of 6.0 during that decade in Manchester was a result of a special goal delivery in October 1867 following a riot which resulted in five being found guilty of murder. In Liverpool the Cornermen only managed to raise the figure to 4.5 in December 1874 in an Assize which had seen 8.0 in November 1870 and 1872. Street violence in Liverpool, where it was a common habit for sailors to wear sheath knives, where drunkenness was rife and violence between Orangemen and Catholics could all combine to produce 185 stabbings in 1856[24] did not need newspaper publicity to produce examples of harsh punishments. However, the publicity given to Liverpool in the national press may have affected the Middlesex figures. In order to prevent the Lancashire disease of violence from becoming virulent in London, deterrent sentences would have been handed down for street violent offences, causing twin peaks in October 1874 and January 1875. There is an indication that local publicity concerning the High Rip in the Autumn of 1886 led to the Winter Assize figure of 4.3 compared to the average figure for the Assize since the beginning of the decade of 2.3.

These figures highlight two main points. First, that preceding newspaper publicity raised the average level of sentence handed down. Only in the case of the aftermath of the Trafalgar Square riot did it have no appreciable effect. Secondly, the effect was more appreciable and dramatic in incidents in London rather than in the provinces. London incidents were reported in national papers, notably, *The Times* and so would be viewed as national incidents. A garotting outbreak in London was a garotting outbreak in Britain. Provincial incidents such as the Scuttlers and the High Rip only received publicity in provincial papers. Judges on circuit would not be readers of the provincial press, having their copy of *The Times* sent up from London, and so would be uninfluenced by their editorials. If the judiciary were in any degree influenced by the press, it was the London press which provided that influence. It was in the sentencing of London criminals, therefore, that the hidden power of the press most clearly exposes itself in the aftermath of street violence scares. As so often with research, the net result is not so much increased knowledge as the increased realisation of the depth of ignorance. To get a fuller explanation of the British criminal justice system wider research would be needed on the personalities and characters of the nineteenth-century judiciary and magistracy. A fuller understanding of judges and magistrates as persons would make it possible to understand further their sentencing policy (especially their susceptibility to media pressure and public opinion) and their whole role as individuals in the machinery of justice.

Notes

1. B. Abel-Smith and R. Stevens, *Lawyers and The Courts: A Sociological Study of the English Law System 1750–1965* (1967), 85–90.
2. C.H.E. Zangerl, 'The Social Composition of the County Magistracy in England and Wales, 1831–87', *Journal of British Studies*, XI, 1, November 1971, 113–125.
3. J.K. Jerome, *Three Men on the Bummel*, (1900).
4. D. Jones, *Crime, Protest, Community and Police in Nineteenth-Century Britain* (1982) 113.
5. Abel-Smith, op.cit., 31.
6. J.P. Dunbabin, 'British Local Government Reform: The Nineteenth-Century and After', *English Historical Review*, 1977, 777–805.
7. W. Nott-Bower, *Fifty-Two Years a Policeman* (1926) 151–2.
8. W. Foulkes (Their Reporter), *A Generation of Judges*, 1886, 147, 84 and 25.
9. E. Foss, *The Judges of England*, vol. 9, 1820–64, (1864).
10. *Dictionary of National Biography*, (1887).
11. Foulkes, op.cit., 28 and 80.
12. *Dictionary of National Biography* (1887).
13. *Dictionary of National Biography* (1887).
14. *Dictionary of National Biography* (1887).
15. Foulkes, op.cit., 55, 79 and 113.
16. Foulkes, op.cit., 2, 10 and 6.
17. C. Fairfield, *A Memoir of Lord Bramwell* (1898), 71.
18. *Dictionary of National Biography* (1887).
19. Arthur Day, *John C.F.S. Day* (1916), 171.
20. *Punch*, 17 June 1882.
21. Day, op.cit., 118.
22. Foulkes, op.ict., 112.
23. Ibid., 84.
24. W.R. Cockroft, 'The Liverpool Police Force, 1836–1902', in S.P. Bell (ed.), *Victorian Lancashire*, (1974).

9. Conclusion

Asa Briggs has observed that, 'Victorian cities were places where problems overwhelmed people'.[1] The people who were so often overwhelmed were the lower orders who had no control over the society which used their labour when it was required and discarded it when it was not. They were consigned to the slum areas of large cities where they dwelt in insanitary hovels, dying by the thousand if ravaged by disease or living out their lives as substandard members of the human species if they survived. Following the Reform Act 1832, Parliament still comprised mainly nobility and gentry but the voters who pulled the puppets' strings were increasingly the middle classes. As the second half of the century progressed these middle classes moved out to the suburbs and segregated themselves from the lower orders. The segregation, however, was not complete, for the middle classes still had to work in the cities and were compelled to travel across the cities daily. Thus they were still touched by the evils of urban living. The living conditions of outcast London were not their living conditions but touched their lives in two important respects. They were forced to travel and work near such conditions and secondly, they were threatened by, if they did not actually experience, contact with the lower orders.

The Great Stink of 1858 from the Thames which was one gigantic flow of industrial and domestic effluent, necessitating the draping of the windows of the Houses of Parliament with curtains soaked in chloride of lime so that MPs might breathe, was a dramatic reminder that the problems emanating from the over-crowded conditions of the lower orders could not always be geographically contained. Sewer gas and smog were visible reminders of an atmosphere in which invisible killers – typhus, cholera and small pox were virulent until the last quarter of the century. As they declined, their contribution to the death rate (then slightly declining) was replaced by tuberculosis, pneumonia and measles. Such diseases, as the middle classes well knew, were not respecters of class. Another aspect of overcrowded urban living which affected the middle-class commuter to town was that of traffic congestion. The walk from the station involved traversing streets which had been designed to take less than half the traffic which now filled them. By the second half of the century the original quagmires which formed the streets were covered in wooden slats which allowed for furious driving in dry conditions and proved dangerously slippery in the wet.

Far more important than the proximity to overcrowded urban conditions, for the middle classes, was the proximity to the lower orders themselves. From the 1830s onwards the middle classes were made increasingly aware of what Disraeli described as the two nations. Booth's study of London in 1889 and Rowntree's study of York in 1901 demonstrated that, despite many areas of material betterment, the concept of two nations was still relevant at the end of the century. The lower orders consituted a perceived major threat to the middle classes who feared the power of the masses should they ever break out socially and geographically. Thus the imposition of order in all its facets on the lower stratum greatly occupied the middle-class mind. Improvement of housing, education, poor-law institutions, recreation, church attendance, etc. were all desired, not for the direct benefit of the recipient lower classes but for the indirect benefit of the middle classes who believed that a slightly more content working class would be more docile and so less threatening.

In addition to any problems posed by the proximity of overcrowded urban conditions and those who lived in such conditions, membership of the middle class posed its own class-generated problems. The life-style and ostentatious display requiring constant employment and periodic promotion were daily threatened by the sack or the onset of illness. Thus the individual member of the middle classes daily faced problems, social, economic and medical, of enormous magnitude. It must be said that street robbery was a threat of minor proportions compared to those other problems which confronted the typical commuter from suburb to town. Nineteenth-century Britain was in a unique position as forerunner in the process of industrialisation and urbanisation and in experiencing the problems that such a process created. Once the threat of political revolution had been neutralised the power elite was secure enough to set about attempting to solve the many social problems. There was a constant tension between those who believed in social control through paternalism and those who looked to the reform of institutions as the answer. As the rate of robbery in England and Wales in 1862 was 3 per 100,000 compared to the present-day figure of 46, the actual number of crimes cannot have posed a very real problem to the individual in the nineteenth century. In certain periods, however, the press gave prominence to street violence so that its magnitude as a real problem was greatly exaggerated.

The new journalism which began in the 1850s was the beginning of a trend which was marked by little differentiation in news content amongst the various newspapers. It was found that certain topics, notably crime, created interest and sold copies. As news is what a newspaper decides to treat as news and topics which have been news in the past are likely to be treated as news again, street violence, once viewed by editors as constituting good copy, was destined to remain as a topic in all newspapers. News that sold copies for one newspaper would do so for the others. Similarly, once one newspaper had ratified an event as news others might accept the ratification and treat the event as independently newsworthy. *The Times* was not part of the new journalism but was probably the leading ratifier to the extent that other newspapers felt the need to report or comment upon the reaction of *The Times* to certain topics and would often reprint *The Times*'s editorials as news in their own right.

For the majority of the population who do not have firsthand knowledge of events then an event only occurs if it is reported in the press and does not occur if it is not. Consequently, with such a small number of actual occurrences to be experienced, street violence only became a problem if the press said it had become a problem and an editorial in *The Times* could be sufficient to classify the problem of street violence as news in other newspapers. This was the arbitrary power of the press to create news and define problems. The sudden reporting of a pheno-menon produced the same reaction as if the phenomenon had suddenly arisen. It has been observed how some of these outbreaks of reporting of events led people to perceive street violence as a problem. At other times, for example, in the cases of the Scuttlers and the Manchester garotters, similar events occurred but were not reported and so from the readership's viewpoint they did not occur and so could not constitute a problem. When perceived as a problem the reports sometimes promp-ted increased action by the police, the judiciary and the legislature, while at other times, for example, in the case of the High Rips in Liverpool in the 1880s, they produced very little reaction.

Herein lies a philosophical problem for the historical researcher. It has to be decided whether actual events or perceived events should be the subject of research. What is history – that which was happening or that which people thought was happening? A dual perception of history is needed so that at any one time we know both the actuality and the perceived reality. It is failure to adopt this dual perception approach which has led to the misuse of criminal statistics by so many researchers of crime. These statistics do tell us a lot about what people thought was happening, but little about what was actually happening in terms of criminal events. This dual perception approach to history results in one conclusion of this work, that while middle-class individuals, the judiciary and the legislature responded to that which was reported as happening, the police, who were closest to actual events in the street and so had greater primary experience, seemed to respond to the events themselves. The police reaction was normally in the form of increasing patrols of uniformed and plainclothes personnel. It rarely resulted in changes at an organisational level, the aftermath of the Trafalgar Square Riot of February 1886 being the exception.

In the case of the Liverpool Cornermen in the 1870s and the High Rips, individuals within the middle classes reacted to the newspaper reports with detached interest as, owing to the geographical location of the violence in rough neighbourhoods, they did not feel directly threatened. It was the metropolitan scares of 1856, 1862, 1867 and 1886 which produced a reaction. Those of 1856 and 1862 led to a fashion in self-protection and all four incidents led to a demand for greater protection to be afforded to innocent citizens by the police.

Once defined as a problem, these perceived events revealed the tensions between the reformist and paternalist opinions in the legislature. The paternalists identified the meddling of the reformers as the cause of the problems and demanded retrogressive action in terms of heightened control and severer punishments. The reformers regarded the inefficient implementation of previous reforms as the cause of failure and demanded a progressive response in the form of greater persistence with reform. The panic legislation of the 1850s and 1860s was the result of the paternalists' arguments gaining temporary dominance during periods of moral panic. The withdrawal of the bill to deal with cases of brutality, following the focusing of press attention on brutality in Lancashire in the 1870s, perhaps demonstrates that the legislature was learning from its previous mistakes. The judiciary were, in all cases, quick to respond to the moral panics and adopt the role of moral entrepreneurs. The passing of exemplary sentences and the general rise in average punishments seemed to be a natural concomitant of all the moral panics studied.

Cohen's model of folk devils and moral panics was derived from observation of mid-twentieth century events yet fits the observed facts of similar nineteenth-century situations. Cohen's model contains several elements all of which may be observed in the nineteenth-century experience of street violence. First, such panics are periodic and form distinct episodes which once finished are often forgotten. Hence, *The Times* could state in 1862 that, 'if street robberies had been at all common ten years ago, we should have infallibly have heard of them',[2] as if their reports, leaders and letters of 1851 and 1856 had never appeared. Secondly, the panics stem from a group of persons being defined as a threat to societal values. The perpetrators of street violence were certainly at odds with the values of the middle-class life of respectability, security and sedentary occupation. Thirdly, the mass media presents the threat in a stylised and stereotyped fashion. This, too, is demonstrable in all the moral panics of the second half of the nineteenth century. Fourthly, as we have seen, the moral barricades are manned by right-thinking people such as editors and politicians and socially-accredited experts pronounce their solutions. Fifthly, stop-gap measures are resorted to, which, in the nineteenth century, involved hurried self-protection by individuals and increased presence of the police until the panic subsided. Lastly, the panics sometimes produce changes in legal and social policy which have more serious and long-lasting repercussions. All six of these elements were clearly present in the moral panics of the second half of the nineteenth century. Cohen's model is therefore applicable over time. The reason why the second half of the nineteenth century witnessed the first of such moral panics is that it was only by that period that the press had developed as a truly mass media capable of acting as a vehicle for such a panic.

Notes

1. A. Briggs, *Victorian Cities* (1968), 22.
2. *The Times*, 26 November 1862.

Index

$$\left(10x^3 - 25x^2\right) - \left(4x + 10\right)$$

$$5x^2(2x-5) - 2(2x-5)$$

$$\left(5x^2 - 2\right)(2x-5)$$